Fireproof

"I wholeheartedly endorse David Hollenbach's new book, *Fireproof*. Filled with exercises designed to help you truly make the best of his powerful teachings around leadership, personal stories to reinforce the point, and powerful quotes that leave you in heavy reflection—this book has everything I love about books in one powerful package. You should definitely grab your copy today and then watch as your life changes from the minute you start reading."

~**Corey Poirier**, Multiple-Time TEDx Speaker Co-Author of the *USA Today / Wall Street Journal* Best Seller, *Quitless*

"When I read Dave's words, "Self-confidence is good, but pride is dangerous," two things happened. First, I got chills and second, I thought, *Those words need to be in Every leadership, manual, textbook and guide that is written.*"

~**Steve Williams**, Investigations Sergeant, California Department of Corrections, Operations Officer, Smith River Fire Rescue

"Have you ever done something you wished you hadn't? Dave Hollenbach's successes and missed-takes help readers grow and create a Grand Strategy with him. A must read for anyone who wants to stop beating themselves up and see the forest (fires) for the trees."

~**Dr. Marissa Pei**, #1 Best-selling Author of *8 Ways to Happiness from Wherever You Are*

"This is very well written and speaks to the reader in ways leadership books aren't known for. David's perspective from years of practical leadership experience is shared in a very humble and unique way. This book will inform even the well-seasoned leader."

~**Robert Riopel**, International Best-selling Author of *Success Left a Clue*

"Throughout life and career there will always be setbacks, tragedies, new opportunities and victories. Hollenbach provides an insightful, practical guide to help illuminate and identify a path toward success in the face of personal and professional challenges, so that we can all achieve our Grand Strategy."

~**Otto Drozd III** Fire Chief, Seminole County Fire Rescue

"Dave tells his leadership journey with brutal honesty, humility, and sincere emotion, detailing failures and successes which will captivate the reader. He provides real world solutions to the difficult problems faced by all leaders. I wish I had his insight when I became a Lieutenant in the FDNY at the age of 30. Well done, Dave. All first responders will benefit from your work. What a great legacy, Dave. You did your father and grandfather proud."

~**FDNY Deputy Chief Austin Horan**, retired

"In this great work Dave Hollenbach guides you on a path to successful leadership, while capturing the essence of our humanity in the process. This book will help you understand that growth comes from knowing yourself and by formulating a plan. David reveals the true nature of humility and service."

~**Hugh Bruder**, Deputy Fire Chief 41-Year
Military and Fire Service Veteran

"David Hollenbach is wise to face squarely into the paradox 'know thyself,' which suggests both past self-knowledge and the ongoing unsettled and unsettling exploration of who we turn out to be. I admire his approach and the way he grounds it in real life."

~**Jeremy Sherman**, Ph.D. Author of *Neither Ghost nor Machine: The Emergence And Nature of Selves.*

"From knowing this brother for many years and knowing his dedication to citizens and the Firehood Family and now seeing his dedication and skills through his knowledge, education and EXPERIENCE as a professional Firefighter and Leader, I would have everyone I know in the profession to not only read his book, but get to know Dave personally! Brother you are doing great things and I am proud of you. Much love and continued success."

~**Tom "Bull" Hill**, Retired firefighter and founder of the Firehood Foundation

FIREPROOF

*Your Grand Strategy for Transforming
Failure into Fuel for Your Future*

DAVID R. HOLLENBACH III

NEW YORK

LONDON • NASHVILLE • MELBOURNE • VANCOUVER

FIREPROOF

Your Grand Strategy for Transforming Failure into Fuel for Your Future

Published in New York, New York, by Morgan James Publishing. Morgan James is a trademark of Morgan James, LLC. www.MorganJamesPublishing.com

Proudly distributed by Ingram Publisher Services.

A **FREE** ebook edition is available for you or a friend with the purchase of this print book.

_____

CLEARLY SIGN YOUR NAME ABOVE

Instructions to claim your free ebook edition:
1. Visit MorganJamesBOGO.com
2. Sign your name CLEARLY in the space above
3. Complete the form and submit a photo of this entire page
4. You or your friend can download the ebook to your preferred device

ISBN 9781631958601 paperback
ISBN 9781631958618 ebook
Library of Congress Control Number: 2021952425

Cover Design by:
Rachel Lopez
www.r2cdesign.com

Interior Design by:
Chris Treccani
www.3dogcreative.net

Morgan James is a proud partner of Habitat for Humanity Peninsula and Greater Williamsburg. Partners in building since 2006.

Get involved today! Visit MorganJamesPublishing.com/giving-back

To my family and friends who have stood by me through tough times and encouraged me to forge ahead, I am eternally grateful.

To my parents who shaped me into the man I am today, thank you for always doing your best to provide direction, support, guidance, and encouragement for me and my brothers.

To my nephews, Aiden and Tristen, I hope you embrace the lessons in this book and find your own versions of success. You have been a tremendous source of inspiration and I thank you for being incredible examples of perseverance regardless of your youth.

To my daughter Isabella, your grace, beauty and kindness have influenced so many, whether you realize it or not. You are a beacon of light to those who are trying to navigate a life full of rough seas. You are and always will be the center of my universe. Therefore, I have dedicated this book to you, Isabella.

The Man in the Arena

It is not the critic who counts; not the man who points out how the strong man stumbles, or where the doer of deeds could have done them better. The credit belongs to the man who is actually in the arena, whose face is marred by dust and sweat and blood; who strives valiantly; who errs, who comes short again and again, because there is no effort without error and shortcoming; but who does actually strive to do the deeds; who knows great enthusiasms, the great devotions; who spends himself in a worthy cause; who at the best knows in the end the triumph of high achievement, and who at the worst, if he fails, at least fails while daring greatly, so that his place shall never be with those cold and timid souls who neither know victory nor defeat.

~**Theodore Roosevelt**, April 23, 1910 in Paris, France[1]

---

1   GoodReads.com, "Theodore Roosevelt > Quotes > Quotable Quote"

CONTENTS

ACKNOWLEDGMENTS

When I began writing this book in 2010, I soon discovered the task was harder than I thought it would be. With that said, it has been more rewarding than I could have ever imagined. This was inspired by the loss of my brother Sean Jacob Hollenbach. He made me want to be better and lead better.

I'm eternally grateful to my parents, MaryAnn, David and Lynn Hollenbach. Without the three of them I would not be who I am today. They taught me discipline, tough love, manners, respect, and so much more that has helped me succeed in life. I truly have no idea where I'd be if they hadn't given me so many different opportunities to grow and the guidance necessary when I needed it.

Many thanks to Chief Otto Drozd, III, who has mentored me and given me direction when the way was not apparent. He has encouraged me, provided me with a hand up when I was knocked down and when I felt as though I was struggling against the bottom of someone's boot. Chief Drozd is the best fire chief I have ever known and a leader I am fortunate to have followed.

Although I wrote of times in my life that were challenging, I believe those dark days tempered my resolve to be a better leader. My time in the fire service wouldn't have been as profound if not for the many men and women I have served with: my father whose footsteps I followed, James Gaut who showed me the power of caring for your people, and Mike Howell who demonstrated consistent leadership and embodied vigilance. The members of the various crews I worked with, in all their iterations are amazing, but the friendships that have endured through my missteps and questionable actions are my most valued. Danita Mundy, you have always been a dear friend and an inspiration.

A very special thanks to Captain Mike Yetter, who has been a friend, a mentor, and often the source of laughs when they were needed most. Thank you for leading me to the well and always being the man in the arena.

Writing a book about the failures in your life is a surreal process. I'm forever indebted to Lana McAra and Randy Peyser for their editorial help, keen insight and ongoing support in bringing my stories to life.

To my family. To Grandma Marie: for always being the consistent voice of reason and source of love. To Uncle Jimmy and Aunt Kelly: for being a second set of parents that got me through the fire academy and many of my growth opportunities. They have influenced who I am in more ways than they will ever know. Aunt Virginia: for always being the caretaker. She sustained me in ways that I never knew that I needed and provided opportunities I otherwise would have never known. Uncle Al: for offering the words of wisdom I desperately required, always with impeccable timing. To my little brother Craig: thank you for letting me know that you had memories of me where I wasn't a complete jerk. I am so thankful to have you in my life. To Georgina Hollenbach: always serving as a solid example for our daughter. She is an amazing example for young women everywhere. Tom Travis: our talks in Mendocino motivated me to study leadership from multiple perspectives, not just mine. He broadened my mind and helped me become a leader that I would follow.

Finally, to all those who have been a part of helping me get this book together: Michael Freeman, Dr. Noel Figueroa, Corey Poirier, Donna Hudepohl, Autumn Clifford, Lori Quint, Katie Schoch, Dawn Briscoe, Jonathan Lawton, Devin Lawton, Nathalie Britt, and Corryne Wheelock. You have my sincere gratitude.

FOREWORD

David Hollenbach is an incredibly gifted writer with a style that is easy to follow.

Fireproof is part biography intertwined with valuable lessons in leadership and important life skills. The material is interesting, incredibly well written and filled with life lessons learned the hard way. It is also an extremely powerful story filled with emotion, sadness and tragedy.

I have both written and read numerous books on leadership, and David's book stands out. He brilliantly tackles the subject in a unique, humble and heartfelt way.

As a firefighter David never lost focus on accomplishing goals, learning from his failures and hardships, and always helping others to achieve their own success. He points out that leadership occupies a dynamic where the more you help others, the more you help yourself, something he calls "selfish-altruism."

His story is an inspirational journey of his own physical and emotional path toward personal growth and success. He took some very unfortunate situations and turned them into valuable life lessons. David openly shares how he gained great wisdom from his own mistakes and poor judgment. He also dealt with PTSD as a fire fighter and struggled with tragic events, including the death of close family members and the divorce of his parents.

People close to him often judged him as a reflection of their preconceived ideas of who he was. They did not see him for the person he actually was. Early on, he recognized that he lacked certain leadership qualities, so he studied leadership and realized the value of a life of humility.

After reading and absorbing David's story, I walked away with more clarity on how to be a better follower and a better leader, the importance of self-leadership. managing relationships, the importance of communication, building healthy habits and dealing with depression.

This story surpassed my highest expectations and was nothing at all like I expected. I don't think there's anyone who wouldn't benefit from reading this book.

~Don D. Mann
New York Times Best-selling Author

INTRODUCTION

After more than thirty years of building my reputation as a trustworthy leader, I messed up and lost it all in a split second. Through my struggle to recover, I developed a passion for helping others avoid that special brand of nightmare. This book began as a compilation of ten years' worth of notes from reading leadership books, working with people in the real world and deep soul searching. When my career ended, my draft of a book on leadership in the fire service suddenly turned into something much more.

Looking back, I realized how I have struggled with impulse control and self-leadership. I also saw how much I have learned over the past ten years, and even more over the last six months. Effective self-leadership is a constant process of improving, stumbling, learning and trying again. Failure is part of the journey. Failing to act because of a fear of failure is still failure.

I learned to keep an open mind and see things for what they are but still question their validity without prejudice. I got clear on who I am and what I stand for. I identified the obstacles that stood in my way and developed my Grand Strategy to break through them.

I also learned that my occupation does not define me. Who I am inside is where my value lies, and that's where I find what I need to help others. I learned to define myself, and set a path that will end up where I want to go, to my end state and my legacy.

Personal, professional, and spiritual development are interdependent. When your goal is to lead people, you must first practice sound, courageous self-leadership. Effective leaders seek opportunities to improve. First, consider where you want to end up, your end goal. What is your purpose for reaching that goal? After disaster strikes, what drives you to get up and get back in the game? You will find answers in the exercises at the end of each chapter. You will also develop your own Grand Strategy to create your life on your terms heading toward your chosen destination—your End State.

The world needs better leaders. Own the moment. Make your life count. This is where to start.

This journey is not for the fainthearted, the person who coasts through life. You will be challenged. You will have your excuses stripped away. You will face the hard questions you have avoided up to now. There are no shortcuts and no work arounds. You will need dedication and commitment. That's what it takes.

You can do this.

The real question is: Are you ready to begin? If not now, when?

CHAPTER 1:

How Do You Define Yourself?

I knew I was in trouble when the cop grabbed the back of my neck and slammed my face into the hood of his patrol car. That was one of those Before-and-After moments. Before, I was rising in the ranks as a firefighter, the son of a leader in the fire service with a bright future ahead of me. After, I was that guy, the person you don't want to be.

In those days, I was working and going to paramedic school, so I didn't have much of a social life. While on winter break, I decided to visit friends and family in south Florida for the week between Christmas and New Year's. I was ready to kick back and have some fun.

On Saturday, December 30, 2000, I spent the afternoon with my old boss and his wife in the relaxed, beachy vibe of the area, catching up and enjoying the day. We had cocktails while he played guitar, and we sang along. When I left there, I went back to my Uncle Jimmy's house where I was staying and had dinner with my aunt and uncle. I had a few more drinks.

Around 9:00 p.m. I decided to go to a local tavern to shoot some pool and hopefully meet up with people I hadn't seen in a while. When I told Uncle Jimmy and Aunt Kelly my plan, they looked skeptical. They followed me to the door. "Are you sure you're okay to drive?" Aunt Kelly asked.

"I'm good," I replied with the wisdom of my twenty-five years. "It's two blocks away. I can always walk if I have too many drinks to drive back."

Eager to start the evening, I headed out. The Saturday night crowd was in full swing when I arrived. I ordered a beer and joined a game of pool. Before long, a beautiful girl sitting at the bar caught my eye. She had curly red hair down her back, freckles and sparkling green eyes. She was small and wearing a yellow sundress with straps that tied in bows on top of her shoulders. A little shy at first, she eventually let me buy her a drink. We hit it off and ended up playing pool for hours. A lot of flirting, a little making out—the night was getting better and better.

Around midnight, her friend came to the pool table and told her, "We're going to Harry's to meet up with Jenny and Tara."

"I'm not ready to leave yet," she said. She glanced at me. "That's just down the road, David. Would you mind driving me over there when we're done with this game?"

Glad that she wanted to stay with me, I said, "Sure." I figured if things didn't go my way at the end of the evening, I could still walk back to my uncle's house.

We went to the second place for a couple of hours, then to a third place.

The third establishment was very close to my uncle's house. It was a small bar that drew an older crowd. People my age would show up after the middle-aged partiers went home. I rarely went there when I was in town because I didn't typically stay out that late.

The tables and bar stools were all taken when we walked in. The bar was an island style in the center, similar to the sitcom *Cheers* with dark woodwork and brass trim. A few tables stood around the edges of the room with a stage and two dueling pianos on one end.

Music was blaring. People had to shout to be heard. A few couples were on the floor near the stage moving to the music. By this time, it was about 2:30 a.m.

We joined some girls standing in a tight cluster at the bar. I had my arm around the red-haired girl, and she was leaning into me. We decided that since it was now December 31, we should toast the New Year. I handed the bartender my credit card and ordered a round of shots for the group of six girls and myself, plus a beer.

After the shots, I went to the restroom.

When I got back, our spot at the bar was empty. I asked the bartender, "Where did those girls go?"

He shrugged. "They left."

I couldn't believe she dumped me like that. What was going on?

"Ready to cash out?" he asked. When I nodded, he handed me a bill of more than $300.

"What's this?" I demanded. "I ordered seven shots and one beer."

He said, "They ordered some more stuff. Your girlfriend said it was cool because you live together."

"I never met any of them before tonight, not even her." I glanced down the slip. They had ordered the most expensive liquor in the place, up to $30 a shot, knocked back a few, then bolted.

My temper rising by the second, I signed the ticket.

By the time I reached my truck, I was so steaming mad that all I could think of was catching them. The street was a dimly lit beach access road with only one direction toward civilization, so I figured they would be easy to find. I put the window down to get some air on my face and peeled out of the parking lot, throwing sand and crushed seashells behind me. The truck fishtailed. I brought it around, my foot still jammed into the floorboards.

The speed limit on that street was 25 m.p.h. The stoplight ahead of me turned yellow. Stomping on the brake, I realized I was doing 70, and that was after slowing down.

Red and blue lights flashed in my rearview. My only thought was a speeding ticket. In my mind, I was okay to drive.

I told the officer what had happened. He said, "Are you a firefighter?" I told him I was. He handed back my license. "Where are you going?"

I pointed toward my uncle's street. "Right there."

"You need to park, and I don't want to see you out again tonight." At that very moment, a second patrol car pulled in behind his. He drew in a long breath and said, "This is not your night. I need your license back."

The driver of that second car was his supervisor who was also the head of the DUI task force.

While they put me through the sobriety tests, I thought they were messing with me because I came through the tests okay. I became confused when they had me put my hands on the hood of the patrol car and patted me down. When the officer told me that they were going to take me in, I jerked around and said, "Really!"

That's when he grabbed my neck and slammed me down. That's when my life changed and never went back.

I spent the first few months of 2001 going through the court process, meeting with the probation officer, required drug testing, community service, AA meetings and substance abuse treatment. My driver's license was restricted to work only. My vehicle was impounded. My family was disappointed, and my career as a firefighter was in jeopardy. My bright future had the lights dimmed out.

I was relieved of duty for more than two months while everything got sorted out. When I returned to shift work in March, I found the atmosphere had changed dramatically. Where I used to be respected and included, now eye contact included unspoken words of condemnation. They assigned me to work with trustees from the local jail picking up trash at the fleet maintenance shop and sweeping the bays in full view of my fellow firefighters. I had to drop out of paramedic school as well.

When I finally got back to fighting fires, I floated from one firehouse to another. Eventually, I was suspended because of the DUI arrest. After my radio was stolen at the scene of a fire, I was terminated for destruction of government property. A few months later, I went to work for a rain gutter and roofing company, fell off a roof and broke my back. I was laid up for the next year, and all I could think about was how to return to the fire service.

Those were tough days for me. I wondered if they would ever end. Now, twenty years later, I can see several important principles I learned at a core level that made me a better leader.

Reputation

My leadership journey began at an early age. I was four years old the first time I slid down the pole at station 41, possibly younger the first time I sat on the fire engine. My father was in the fire service. He was my hero, bigger than life, and I wanted to be just like him. Words like *honor*, *service* and *integrity* meant a lot in my family.

I knew I was born to be a firefighter. Throughout school, I worked hard and stayed out of trouble. I had a straight path ahead of me, and I was on my way. Here's a brief rundown of where I was when I ran into my first Growth Opportunity.

1993 I joined the United States Navy.

1996 I enrolled in EMT school.

1997 I joined the volunteer fire department in Martin County, Florida, and ended up at an all-volunteer station in Jensen Beach.

1998 I graduated from Indian River Fire Academy.

1999 A large fire department in Central Florida hired me. I worked my way up the ranks holding positions in Training, Special Operations, and Administration with the bulk of my service being in Operations.

When I headed to South Florida on winter break after Christmas of 2000, I had everything going for me. I never dreamed that before New Year 2001 rang in, my career would have a giant question mark hanging over it. A brief lapse in judgement will destroy a stellar reputation in seconds.

"A brief lapse in judgement will destroy a stellar reputation in seconds."

Small Decisions Make a Big Difference

During that fateful night on the town, I made a series of poor decisions that led me to a crisis. At the time they seemed like small things—whether to walk the two blocks to the tavern or drive, whether to take a pretty girl up the street to meet her friends or politely decline, whether to cut my losses on the bar tab and head home or rush out in a rage to get some kind of justice. With a change in just one choice, that night would have ended much differently.

Life's decisions are like shooting an arrow at a target. You must take into account elevation, distance, wind, humidity, obstructions, the weight of the point and the shaft as well as the tension of the string. If your aim is off a fraction of an inch, the arrow will miss the bullseye. Once the arrow has left the bow, you no longer have control. It's going to fly and land where it will. When you miss the mark, all you can do is adjust your aim and take another shot.

All of history's greatest leaders experienced tremendous failures. Those tough times might even be what shaped them. Failure teaches you two things: (1) how resilient you are and (2) humility is a good thing. No matter how good you think you are or how high you have risen, you could still fall short. Failure stings less when you are humble.

I read "The Man in the Arena"[2] by Theodore Roosevelt whenever I wanted to reinforce the lessons I learned those many years ago.

The Man in the Arena

It is not the critic who counts; not the man who points out how the strong man stumbles, or where the doer of deeds could have done them better. The credit belongs to the man who is actually in the arena, whose face is marred by dust and sweat and blood; who strives valiantly; who errs, who comes short again and again, because there is no effort without error and short-

---

2   Ibid.

coming; but who does actually strive to do the deeds; who knows great enthusiasms, the great devotions; who spends himself in a worthy cause; who at the best knows in the end the triumph of high achievement, and who at the worst, if he fails, at least fails while daring greatly, so that his place shall never be with those cold and timid souls who neither know victory nor defeat ~Theodore Roosevelt, April 23, 1910, Paris, France

When you fall, dust yourself off and keep going. Figure out what you did wrong and promise yourself you'll never do that again. If you don't learn from your mistakes, you are doomed to repeat them.

Define Yourself or Someone Else Will Define You

From all appearances, that December night in 2000 ruined my life. I ended up on my couch with a broken back and in a deep depression, my life purpose crushed into the sand. One day my Uncle Al called to ask how I was doing. During the conversation, he told me, "The measure of a man is not the mistakes he has made, but what actions he took to correct those mistakes."

If you allow failure to define you, then you are a failure. Leaders define themselves. They do not quit because of some detour or stumbling block along the way. They learn what they can from the experience and take the next step in the right direction. Every single day, I still push forward to improve myself. With every setback comes an opportunity to become better.

"Leaders define themselves."

Everyone Experiences Failure

When you dare to achieve greatness, you put yourself at higher risk for failure than those who are satisfied with mediocrity. Leaders always deal with setbacks. Not everyone will approve of your methods. Some will find fault no matter how brilliant or circumspect you are. Stand tall and persevere. NEVER QUIT! Every successful leader perseveres in the face of adversity.

I also learned that failure affects those closest to you—your friends and family. After three years of trying to get back in, I was finally reinstated into the fire service in 2004. The following year I was promoted to engineer. I thought my years of humiliation were over. Unfortunately, I was wrong.

When my father retired from the State Fire Marshal's Office in 2005, people in high positions all over Florida travelled to congratulate him at the luncheon in his honor. They stood up and spoke of how he helped shape their careers, how he influenced their lives and his many contributions to the fire service. I had no idea my father was a man of such great renown and reputation. He never once bragged about his achievements. I had no idea how humble he was.

After the event, I felt proud standing with him. Well-wishers came by to shake his hand and say nice things. When they finished congratulating him, many of them looked over at me and remarked about my drinking. One of them said, "Hey, Hollenbach, want a drink?" Something inside me curled up a little tighter and more painful with every comment. My father tried to laugh off their remarks, and that hurt me worse than anything.

I am David Hollenbach III. I have my father's name, as he has my grandfather's. My shortcomings were not private. They were directly linked to my father's legacy because I have his name. That day, I decided I would not allow my actions to tarnish my father's name any more. I committed myself to becoming the best part of my father's fire service legacy, not the stain I was then.

No formal leadership development program or mentoring program existed in my fire department at that time, but some officers mentored people on their crews. Whenever I worked with men I respected, I soaked up as much as I could from them. I studied hard. I trained hard. Unfortunately, that wasn't enough.

Three years later, when I was promoted to lieutenant, I quickly realized that I lacked the qualities of a leader. I had rank, but the crew at that station was established and somewhat senior. Two of my crew members had more time on the job than me and more experience. Fortunately, the good people on that crew helped me develop.

One of my best friends, Mike Yetter, was also a student of leadership. He was always available to discuss work issues with me. Mike was an officer with Miami Dade Fire Rescue, a former Army Infantryman and all-around great guy. He recommended several books to me. Once I got a taste of leadership training, I developed a thirst for more and my quest began.

I devoured books on leadership. I searched the Internet for leadership development programs hoping I could find something that I could use in my station. During my quest, I found a video of Colonel Art Athens speaking in front of a group of Midshipmen[3] where he tells a story about one of his mentors. Fresh out of officer training, his mentor was assigned command of a Marine Corps unit with a seasoned gunnery sergeant as second in command. The young officer asked his gunnery sergeant one question: "Given both of our levels of experience, why would you follow me?" The

---

3   USNALeadConf. "USNA LC09 - Col. Arthur Athens, USMC (Ret.)" YouTube. com. Aug 26, 2013. Accessed Aug 29, 2021.

gunny replied that he and the platoon would be watching him to answer three questions based on his actions:

1. Do you know your job or are you striving hard to learn it?
2. Will you make the hard-but-right decisions, even if it costs you personally?
3. Do you care as much about us as you care about yourself?

These questions are the Three C's of Leadership: Competence, Courage, and Compassion. Colonel Athens focused the rest of his lecture on the third C, Compassion.

Leadership isn't about being in charge. It's about working hard to ensure your team's success. The skills required to be an effective leader can be learned. However, using those skills takes courage and commitment. The challenges are real, relentless and inevitable. Sometimes, they hit you out of nowhere.

Great leaders know that excellence is not a destination. Excellence is a path, a calling. Great leaders accept no excuses for mediocrity. On Day One they stand out. They step up and say, "You can count on me." They make a decision to earn their place of honor and keep earning it every day.

But even more, they realize their good name is more valuable than any number of bugles or badges or patches or medals. I have my father's name and my grandfather's name. I am their legacy. My name means something to me. I want it to mean something long after I am gone, and I want every member of my team to leave the same kind of legacy.

When you develop this level of trust with your people, they will go far beyond what they imagine they are capable of. So will you.

---

*"Great leaders know that excellence is not a destination.
It is a path, a calling."*

My Growth Opportunity seemed like a string of bad luck from mixing it up with the wrong pretty girl to the head of the DUI task force showing up at precisely the wrong moment. In reality, my "bad luck" happened because I didn't have a defined plan for my life and my career. I didn't have a Grand Strategy.

Your Grand Strategy

In Linda Kulman's book *Teaching Common Sense: The Grand Strategy Program at Yale University*, she writes about the program established in 2000. The Grand Strategy Program was created by professors who were seasoned leaders in the real world—John Lewis Gaddis, Robert A. Lovett, Paul M. Kennedy, J. Richardson Dilworth and Charles Hill. They wanted to develop leaders who could think on their feet and use common sense.

Students in the program studied different philosophies and various methods of strategic thinking. After mastering the foundational material, they were then involved in scenarios where they had to make big decisions using what they had learned. They practiced making fast decisions to achieve practical outcomes.

Linda Kulman quotes Henry Kissinger as stating,

I think one of the empty spaces in our country . . . is the study of strategic issues," he commented. "We lack [the] preparation of a young leadership group . . . That is, how you assemble the issues that are relevant to national decision making and develop a habit of thought that you get to automatically. The American tendency is to wait for a problem to arise and then to overwhelm it with resources or with some pragmatic answers. But what you need is a framework of decisions that helps you understand where you're trying to go.[4]

A Grand Strategy defines big picture actions that may or may not be used in order to achieve big picture goals. This approach is typically reserved for policies and actions of national leaders with the intent to maintain, achieve, or improve domestic and foreign affairs. When allowing contingencies for the responses of other nations, they reached their desired outcomes faster and with less collateral damage.

"A Grand Strategy defines big picture actions that may or may not be used in order to achieve big picture goals."

In my quest to learn more about leadership, I came across this idea of a Grand Strategy and wondered, what if people had a Grand Strategy? What if you saw your life from the highest vantagepoint and took the same approach as nations when setting up a plan to achieve your goals? When you think in these terms, you can look at contingencies that you'd never see on a smaller scale.

The first step in building a Grand Strategy is to identify the End State you want. Keep in mind that the rewards for a life well spent are a result, not an End State. Rewards might include a nice retirement income, a house on the shore and a fishing boat at your

---

4   Linda Kulman & Henry Kissinger, *Teaching Common Sense: The Grand Strategy Program at Yale University.*

disposal. An End State is being a great leader who ensures the success of your people.

When preparing a Grand Strategy, think of it as a military operation. Once you determine your ultimate destination, you set up multiple roads to get there. You also plan for multiple modes of transportation. If a bridge falls to the enemy, you have other routes lined out. If a dam breaks and washes out the roads, you have alternate methods to reach the destination. Contingencies are essential for success because you can count on the need for course corrections along the way. Everyone has Personal Detours at times. Often, when you least expect them. You will need to make fast decisions with the least collateral damage possible.

What Is Your Desired End State?

A leader's desired End State must be broad and loosely defined. Use general terms during the early part of the build because you cannot know what the future holds. You might be in medical school with the goal of being a doctor. After a few years in private practice, you might decide you would rather do something else. You might go into law enforcement or decide you would rather try your hand in the arts or politics or open a small business.

Your occupation, the thing that allows you to pay your bills, is not important in the long run. How you influence people around you and add value to their lives is your desired End State.

"Your occupation, the thing that allows you to pay your bills, is not important in the long run."

You followed the men and women who came before you. Who are you leading? What example are you setting? One day someone will write down a few words to read in front of those family members who survive you. They will stand up and talk about how you touched their lives. You are writing those words in their hearts and their minds right now. What are you writing?

Action Step 1: Determine your End State.

What is your desired End State? What do you want others to remember about you when you are gone? A great exercise that I have used many times is to write out your own eulogy. First, you would write one as if you died yesterday. Second, you write one as if you have accomplished everything you have dreamed of accomplishing. Write it as though someone you have yet to meet is your dearest friend, mentor, or a mentee twenty years from now who is going to read it to all of the people you care about.

_____

_____

_____

_____

_____

_____

CHAPTER 2:

Where Are You Going?

After identifying your End State, what you might call your legacy, you are ready to work backward and set up your strategy for achieving it. Similar to building a house, once you have your plan for the finished product, you will now go back and draw up blueprints for the framing, electrical, plumbing, etc. Under each of those headings are steps to complete them.

A leader's gauge of success is the success of those they lead. Looking at your End State, how could you achieve the greatest impact on your team? Would you mentor them, develop training programs, write books and hold seminars? Would you lead by example, so others will want to emulate you? Even if you want to do all of the above, you still begin with one step, one focus.

In your current situation, what action would allow you to achieve maximum impact for the energy you have available? Say you have a passion for helping underprivileged youth. If you have one evening a week available, how can you can maximize your time and get the most results? Maybe you need to start off by building trusting relationships, so you play basketball at the community center every Tuesday night. Maybe you want to establish yourself as a mentor, so you hold free Saturday seminars on relevant topics such as how to get and keep a job or how to obtain a high school diploma after dropping out.

"What action would allow you to achieve maximum impact for the energy you have available?"

When you have a specific end in mind, you can make incremental advances toward that goal and stay engaged for the long haul. Even if you have only one evening a week, when you make that one evening count for as much as possible, you will have motivation to keep going.

Expect bumps in the road to happen. However, during those difficult times, avoid catastrophic thinking where you mentally cycle through dreadful scenarios and end up feeling defeated. If you fall into that trap, you will become an obstacle within yourself. Yes, reflect on various situations and come up with solutions, but don't let potential problems slow you down.

This is why studying philosophical and strategic literature is the first component of Yale's Grand Strategy program. Successful people in the past confronted many obstacles. Not only did they overcome those problems, but they also wrote about how they did it. Learning from them is a critical factor for success. Later, I will show how ancient wisdom has a clear connection to modern psychology. If you don't see the connection in the next paragraph now, you will later.

In *A Man's Search for Meaning*, Viktor Frankl says the human existence has a "tragic triad" of pain, guilt, and death.[5] He also talks about tragic optimism:

> An optimism in the face of tragedy and in view of the human potential which at its best always allows for: (1) turning suffering into a human achievement and accomplishment; (2) deriving from guilt the opportunity to change oneself for the better; and (3) deriving from life's transitoriness an incentive to take responsible action.[6]

In spite of death's certainty, in spite of life's pain, in spite of whatever negative situation you find yourself in, finding your purpose is imperative. We all must define our purpose for ourselves because it is different for everyone, and yet it is the same. As Marcus Aurelius wrote in *Meditations*, "We all exist for one another." As we add value to ourselves, we are better able to add value to others. This universal truth is found throughout the world's religions and in the works of history's greatest thinkers. How we apply our energy sets us apart from one another, and while it sets us apart, it also brings us together.

---

5   Viktor E Frankl, *Man's Search for Meaning.*
6   Ibid.

> *"As we add value to ourselves, we are better able
> to add value to others."*

Part of Frankl's work is Socratic dialogue or attitude modification where the therapist asks particular questions guiding people to perceive their own negative attitudes and develop a more positive outlook with the goal of entering the path to a fulfilled life.[7]

Frankl identified three main ways of finding meaning in life:

- Creative Values: making a difference in the world through our actions, our work or our creations
- Experiential Values: experiencing truth, beauty and love
- Attitudinal Values: adopting a courageous and exemplary attitude in situations of unavoidable suffering[8]

In *Leadership in Turbulent Times*, author Doris Kearns Goodwin writes about the defining moment of Abraham Lincoln's political career.

As one of the chief architects and advocates of Illinois' expansive dreams, Lincoln received the lion's share of the blame for the ensuing catastrophe. The crushing debt crippled the state, destroyed its credit rating for years, and deterred new pioneers from settling in Illinois. Land values plummeted, thousands lost their homes, banks and brokerage houses closed down. Acknowledging that he was "no financier," Lincoln shouldered responsibility for the crisis and paid a heavy

---

7   Ameli, M., & Dattilio, F. M. (2013). "Enhancing cognitive behavior therapy with logotherapy: Techniques for clinical practice". *Psychotherapy*. 50 (3): 387–391.

8   Viktor Frankl, *The Doctor and the Soul*.

price for that admission. His belief in himself shaken, he announced his retirement from the state legislature at the end of the current term.

Most troubling to Lincoln was the realization that his reputation had been compromised. He had promised the people during his first run for office that if elected, he would support any law providing dependable roads and navigable rivers so the poorest and most thinly populated communities could thrive. That pledge, which he considered binding upon his honor, reputation, and character, had not been fulfilled. The burdens he had sought to lift from the people had instead been multiplied.[9]

Lincoln had to repair what was lost, to reconstruct both his private and his public life. Step by step, this was to become the task of better than a decade.[10]

Oprah was fired from her first reporting job. FDR contracted polio, but he didn't let his resulting disability keep him out of the White House. Twenty-eight-year-old J.K. Rowling left Portugal to escape domestic violence and became a single mother with a three-month-old daughter. She lived in a flat in Scotland, on welfare, hopeless and suicidal, writing a fantasy novel while wondering if she and her little girl would end up homeless.

Nelson Mandela spent twenty-seven years in prison. What few people know is that Mandela refused a conditional release in

---

9   Doris Kearns Goodwin, *Leadership: In Turbulent Times*, 98.
10 Ibid.

1985[11] after serving more than twenty years. He stayed strong in his purpose regardless of what others said about him or tried to coerce him to do.

These leaders and multiplied thousands like them adopted a courageous and exemplary attitude in situations of unavoidable suffering. They experienced truth, beauty and love, and they made a difference in the world. So, can you and I.

Who Am I?

When I made the decision to become the best part of my father's legacy, I knew I would have to make some changes. I went into research mode and read book after book. In my quest to get better answers, I realized I needed to ask better questions.

Most people ask the question, "What should I do to reach my goal?" The Grand Strategy process begins with a much better question: "Who do I need to be?"

"Who do I need to be?"

Whether you start your Grand Strategy as a raw recruit or a Captain, every step up involves the same question: Who do I need to be as I engage this new level of leadership? When you are a strong leader, you go through a constant process of strengthening your core belief about who you are.

What fills the innermost sphere at the center of your being? A strong core essence will give you the strength of Mandela and the

---

11   D.L. Chandler, "How Nelson Mandela refused freedom in 1985 before he walked out of jail in 1990."

resilience of Lincoln. Who you are is the juice that powers every-thing you do. Your core essence determines what kind of leader you are.

Does that mean you have to be perfect? Fortunately, no. Every-one has room to grow. When you know what's inside you—flaws and all—you can use tools to make the shifts, to release your lim-itations and to let go of self-defeating behaviors. You can, in real and practical ways, define yourself.

After all I went through during those years of my Growth Opportunity, I had enough self-blame to fill an ocean liner. Facing myself was one of the hardest things I've ever done, but it was the first step to turning my life around and heading in a positive direc-tion. I had to fully embrace what my Uncle Al told me: "The mea-sure of a man is not the mistakes he has made, but what actions he took to correct those mistakes."

Transparency and vulnerability are foundational qualities for broadening your influence, but first you have to be transparent and vulnerable with yourself, your harshest critic. Instead of shying away from a long, painful look in a dark mirror, I realized the dark mirror was my ticket out of the hole I had dug for myself. I learned the difference between healthy humility and relentless self-reproach.

Humility allows you to let down your guard and connect to peo-ple through your shared humanity, where you encourage each other and say, "We're all in this together." On the other hand, feeling like a loser stifles your ability to lead and destroys your influence.

Everyone makes mistakes. Some get up and dust themselves off. They step back into the arena and keep making progress. Those people are leaders.

Self-Leadership

When a Growth Opportunity shows up, strong leaders ask themselves, "How can I add value to myself, so I can add value to others?" This is a continuous process where you level up through internal growth to thrive at that next level, then do it again and again. Up leveling might mean more education, coaching with someone or becoming an apprentice. You might need to let go of faulty or archaic views about yourself that stop you from reaching the next level. That is where courageous self-leadership comes into play. If you can't lead yourself to respond as you expect your own role models to do, how can you expect others to respect and follow you?

Self-Awareness

Almost 3,000 years ago, 3 of the 147 Delphic Maxims were inscribed on a column in the forecourt of the Temple of Apollo at Delphi in Ancient Greece. Legend says the Oracle at Delphi wrote the first one: "Know thyself." The Oracle of Delphi was Pythia, high priestess of the Temple of Apollo in the 8th century B.C.[12] Self-awareness is a very old concept. It is still around today because it is true.

In order to practice self-leadership, you must know yourself. You must also know how others perceive you and whether they trust you. People naturally gravitate toward leaders who are self-aware, who work hard at improving themselves and improving others. When you lack self-awareness, your communication leaves people feeling uncertain about whether they can trust you. If they don't trust you, they won't follow you for very long.

---

12   Gabriel H. Jones, "Pythia," *World History Encyclopedia.*

Selfish-Altruism

Leadership occupies a dynamic where the more you help others, the more you help yourself. I call this Selfish-Altruism. For the purposes of this study, I define altruism as selfless giving without wanting anything in return. Selfish-Altruism is giving of yourself to support the success of your team.

Selfish-Altruism has roots in Stoic philosophy. Marcus Aurelius summed up Selfish-Altruism quite succinctly when he said, "What is bad for the hive is bad for the bee." If you were a bee, you would work tirelessly to add real and genuine value to the hive. Your efforts would benefit you because you are part of the hive.

Egoistic-altruism, on the other hand, is creating an illusion that you are giving selflessly when you actually want to score points of some kind, such as a celebrity visiting the scene of a disaster as a photo-op for their Instagram account. No matter how good an egoistic-altruist looks, they soon show their true colors with self-serving decisions and "playing the game" to climb the ladder.

Selfish-Altruism is related to personal development where you add value to yourself to become more of an asset to your team. As you help individual members of your team grow stronger, your team becomes more effective. What is good for the hive is good for the bee.

What is good for the hive is good for the bee.
~ Marcus Aurelius

Communication

Communication begins with trust. When you treat people with respect, and you are consistent in making decisions for the greater good, your team will develop a desire to understand your instructions. When you are consistently committed to helping them be successful, they will realize the advantage of paying attention and trusting your judgment, even when they don't understand why you're making a certain call. You will break through the sound barrier that many leaders encounter when their team doesn't seem to hear them.

Trust goes both ways. As they learn to trust you, you learn to trust them. This bond of trust will allow you to take them further than they ever imagined. As the leader, you know the possibilities and the potential. With trust, you will be able to push out the boundaries of what is possible.

Effective communication is foundational to this level of trust and the advancement of the people you lead. While you're framing your instructions, here are some questions to consider:

- How am I being received?
- Do they understand what I'm saying?
- Do they understand my expectations?
- Is my tone making them feel different than what I want them to feel?
- Do they understand my intentions for how I'm speaking to them?
- Do they know my primary goal is to ensure their success?
- Do they feel comfortable asking me questions to get clear on what I want?
- Can they accurately restate my directive?

Effective communication comes down to a legitimate, genuine care for the people you are leading. When they trust that you have the best intentions for their success and the team's success, they will hear you and follow through.

For many years, I wanted to be a well-respected leader in the fire service. Because of my past failures and personal insecurities,

I sometimes allowed doubt to take down my energy and affect my motivation. Those doubts would materialize in negative self-talk where I would question my value. Why would anyone follow me, especially if they know more than me, have fought more fire than me, extricated more people from vehicles than me, ran more calls, saved more people, and on and on. What did I have to offer them?

My answer: I can help them achieve their version of success. In order to do that, I must effectively communicate with them in a way that builds trust. Sometimes that means humility and vulnerability. Sometimes that means blunt honesty and making the hard decisions. When team members realize they can depend on you to take action for the greater good, they will trust you more and more over time.

"I can help them achieve their version of success."

This is especially true when they see you working hard to develop your own capabilities, so you can add value to the team. Your purpose links into their self-improvement goals, and part of their success is belonging to a team that makes the world a better and safer place.

With this positive momentum, the team feels more confidence, and they become even more committed to following their leaders. Some will do additional work to develop themselves, so they have more to offer the group. The team feels an upward surge toward greater excellence. They see that self-development is worthwhile, so they work harder and with even more commitment. The leadership experiences tremendous rewards in both team performance and the development of each member.

By adding value to yourself, you create a triple win: The team benefits. Each team member benefits. You, the leader, benefit. This is Selfish-Altruism.

Your End State

For some in vocations such as politics, the fire service or law enforcement, your End State would typically mean rising in the ranks while teaching and mentoring people within your department. As your legacy, you want to leave your stamp on the culture and overall performance of your team. In my coaching program, I've seen many people who naturally gravitate toward this. However, some people might not want the pressure and responsibility of higher positions. They might prefer to motivate others by setting a stellar example. Some create virtual coaching programs or YouTube videos. Others step out of public view and write books.

During my years as Battalion Chief, I saw experienced lieutenants who were excellent mentors for new people coming in. They also gave me valuable insights as their leader. Those men found their sweet spot, serving where they were happy while also spreading their influence both up and down within the department. Many of these men taught classes on their days off. They spread their influence in ways that felt comfortable for them. I have a lot of respect for them because they added tremendous value to the department in many ways.

Leadership has more than one direction. You can inspire those at higher levels, support and encourage your co-workers and team members while also teaching those who are new to the job.

"Leadership has more than one direction."

Your leadership focus might have nothing to do with your career, but develop from a passion you once considered a sideline, such as an accountant who loves construction. After retirement, he might head up teams with Habitat for Humanity, teaching volunteers. The possibilities are limitless.

When choosing your method of influence, consider how you want to anchor your End State into your daily life. Where is your sweet spot? How would you like to pass along your wisdom and experience, so others can go further?

- Do you want to be in the limelight or behind the scenes?
- Do you thrive in positions of authority or do you find high levels of responsibility too stressful?
- Would you rather work one-on-one or with groups?
- Do you feel comfortable with public speaking?
- How can you reach your End State while enjoying a good quality of life for you and your family?

One of my coaching clients was in law enforcement. I'll call her Amelia (not her real name). She saw her career progressing in a fairly typical way with a promotion to Investigator followed by a Bachelor's degree, promotion to lieutenant and a Master's degree. She saw the potential to be Police Chief in fifteen years and created a timeline for that to happen.

She broke her fifteen-year goal into yearly, quarterly, monthly, weekly and daily action steps. When she encountered an area where she needed help, she would look for a mentor, a program or counseling to help her across the rough patch. This is fairly standard in goal setting, but the Grand Strategy has an added emphasis on building your life around your End State, whether on the job or not.

Be Strategic in Reaching Your Goals

To move along faster in reaching your goals, look for commonalities. When I was in the fire service, I worked hard to learn as much as I could, so I could mentor and coach others. I learned through reading, enrolling in programs and classes as well as working with coaches and counselors. I found that I loved helping others live better and do better both personally and in their career. When I left the fire service, I still had that passion to help others burning within me. What I found was that my reach expanded to include law enforcement, first responders, military personnel and more. The principles are valid and effective no matter what area of work you might be in.

The same is true on a personal level. For example, if you're having difficulty in your relationships, you might need to improve your communication skills. Better communication will also help you as a team leader, as a parent and in many other areas of your life. Personal development digs deep into how you see yourself, how you see the world and how other people see you—which takes you right back to self-leadership, where the journey begins.

Leadership principles hold true even if your path to your End State is unusual, as it was for Tom "Bull" Hill, retired firefighter and president of The Firehood Foundation. Bull is well known for "The March of the Bull" from the Zero Mile Marker in Key West, Florida, to the capitol in Tallahassee, a distance of more than 640 miles. "The March" began as a promise to a brother firefighter dying of cancer. At the time, Florida's Worker's Compensation insurance had no provision for cancer, although firefighters are often exposed to carcinogens and many do end up with cancer.

Bull was so moved by his friends' plight and the struggle of their families that he began to develop a plan to walk the perimeter of Florida in memory of these men, carrying a backpack with the helmet shields of some who had died. People began connecting with Bull, asking him to carry the helmet shields of their loved ones on his backpack. Others urged him to raise awareness and fundraise. The movement grew. He received shields from families in other states, including the shield of an FDNY firefighter who gave all on 9/11. Soon, "The March of the Bull" became a reality.[13]

Bull Hill was instrumental in policy changes at the state level. He also helped many people in need and continues to do so. His impact after retiring is in another category compared to the contributions during his career—and he helped thousands during his career. Bull's End State is a legacy of honoring those who made great sacrifices and inspiring others to hold true and keep the faith. Bull's story is a fine example of how someone took the grief and pain of a situation and turned it into a way to bless others and effect positive change.

Action Step 2: Write down your goals and a timeframe.

Below is space to begin your list of long-term goals. Break them down into short-term goals and action steps. The accompanying workbook has more space for writing and more questions to help you along. If you don't have the workbook yet, now is a good time to order one for more help in completing your Grand Strategy.

Long-Term Goals _____

_____

_____

_____

---

13 Hear the complete interview at www.HollenbachLeadership.com/from-embers-to-excellence-podcast/interview-with-tom-bull-hill-retired-firefighter-and-president-of-the-firehood-foundation

_____
_____
_____
_____
_____
_____
_____

Short-Term Goals

_____
_____
_____
_____
_____
_____
_____

CHAPTER 3:

What Do You Stand For?

The most important trait you have as a leader is a clear understanding of who you are and what you stand for—which
some people call your core values. Take a moment and let this roll
around in your mind. What core values do your actions reveal?
How do you appear to your family, your team members and people
who happen to cross your path? How are you showing up in your
relationships, your finances, managing your health and setting up
your quality of life? Do your actions line up with what you claim
are your ideals?

Leaders are consistent. The first step toward consistent action
is to find out the answer to that one big question: Why? Why did
George Washington spend a harsh winter with his men at Val-
ley Forge when his mansion was only a couple of days away via

horseback? Why did Gandhi go on hunger strikes for weeks at a time while everyone else on his team had plenty to eat? Why did Martin Luther King Jr. take great personal risks during volatile times? Great leaders know what they stand for, and they stand strong no matter what.

Every individual has an idea about qualities that make a great leader, such as honest, brave, intelligent, loyal, fair, enthusiastic, unselfish, decisive, adaptive, a good coach, credible, a good communicator, an excellent listener, dependable and maybe even persuasive or inspiring. Those are all admirable traits that you might want in your life, but unless your actions demonstrate them, they are merely wishful thinking.

Core Values

When you know your values, many gray areas disappear. You have a clear sense of which actions line up with those values, so you can make better decisions.

"When you know your values, many gray areas disappear."

Recently, I brainstormed with my fourteen-year-old daughter, Isabella, to fashion an anchoring statement. I wanted something that I can say to myself when I reach an ethical crossroads, and the same for her. We fashioned a set of core values for ourselves to help us stay clear on our purpose and stay true to our sense of self.

To make it personal, we asked, "What are the characteristics of someone we would want to work for or follow?" We were looking for qualities we admire in several leaders. Drawing from military web sites and other resources, we started with twelve words, narrowed them down and dialed them in until we had a short list that was easy to remember and relevant to both her and me.

As we considered each word, we discovered that many of them are synonyms. Starting at the top of the list, we picked one value we liked and compared it to every word from that point on. If another word topped our current favorite, we went with the new word until something else beat it. This way we came up with our top four values.

Substantiate your final list by examining major decisions in your life to see if those values made an impact on your actions. For example, someone who quits a good job to become an entrepreneur might have a core value of autonomy. They might have a deep need to be their own boss, even if it means a cut in pay or loss of hard-earned rank. Knowing the high value they put on autonomy would help that person's decision-making process when opportunities comes up in the future.

Your choices are solid indicators of what your true core values really are. Keeping this in mind will help you avoid the pitfall of making an academic listing about what you think a good leader should be, rather than identifying the values driving your life.

What about you? What values guide your actions? Your titles don't define you. Your career doesn't. Your net worth doesn't. The accolades you receive from others do not define you.

Who you are at the core comes out through your actions. Are you after money? Do you chase notoriety through flashy deeds? Do you work all the time because promotion and position drive you? Can you say that your actions represent a leader you would want to follow? Would you want your children to emulate your behavior?

If you see leadership as a way to gain prestige or respect or some other vanity, you will never be associated with great leadership. You will never be satisfied, and you will never be truly happy. That is a certainty because the primary focus of a strong leader is the success of the people they lead. People follow others because they believe they will be better for having done so.

"People follow others because they believe they will be better for having done so."

If honest introspection confirms that you value a certain quality, such as courage, yet your behavior shows that you sometimes cave in under pressure, this could be a sign that you have a negative mindset about yourself or how the world works. Some past trauma or conditioning instilled a belief that you don't have what you need to be your best self. This is why coaching is so important. Someone with training and experience can point up these discrepancies in a safe and helpful way, so you can find out what's going on and correct the problem.

When your behavior reveals that you are sidestepping your core values, it does not mean you are a bad person or that you are broken. Instead, it is a sign that you need to unravel some hidden problems. Everyone has dark places inside. Strong leaders are willing to engage a coach or counselor and do the hard work, so they can approach life from a stronger and healthier place. This happens at every level of growth whenever you expand to the next level to fulfill a greater role than you had before.

When your actions consistently align with your values, you can fully embrace your leadership qualities and build trust with those around you. This is integrity.

Whenever I think of integrity, I go back to when I was a kid and my dad telling me that at the end of the day our integrity is all we have. He explained it using a Navy term: Watertight Integrity. Navy warships are constructed in such a way that each compartment can be sealed off from the rest of the ship. This allows it to remain afloat and functioning if a torpedo, missile, mine, or other projectile were to rip a hole in her side. We all have faults. We all have taken damage from the actions of others and acts of our own doing. If your integrity remains intact at your core, you are more capable of continuing on with your mission—doing what you know is right.

While integrity appears in most lists as a value, it affects all your other values by bringing in the idea of consistency. When you have integrity, what you say matches your actions. Who you are deep inside lines up with your decisions, and what others say about you also matches those same values. Integrity is consistency through and through.

> *"Stop talking about what the good person is like,*
> *and just be one."*
> **—Marcus Aurelius**[14]

Stoicism

When I was reading book after book on leadership, I found many references to Stoic philosophy. At first I ignored them, but when I explored the website of the United States Naval Academy, I found a link to the Vice Admiral James B. Stockdale Center for Ethical Leadership. Admiral Stockdale intrigued me. I wanted to know why the Navy named their leadership school after him.

---

14   Marcus Aurelius, *Meditations* 10:16

Searching online, I found a transcript of a talk Admiral Stockdale gave to some Marine Corps pilots where he told the story of how he was shot down at the beginning of the Vietnam War. He spent the next seven years as a prisoner of war. As the ranking officer in captivity, he was tortured and endured the loss of many of his men.

According to Admiral Stockdale, years earlier he was introduced to Epictetus, a Greek slave who was freed in ancient Rome. Epictetus became one of history's greatest Stoic philosophers. He taught about integrity, self-management and personal freedom. He demanded that his students thoroughly examine two central ideas: (1) volition and (2) the correct use of impressions.[15] Stockdale frequently studied Epictetus's writing, "The Discourses" and its abridged version, "The Enchiridion," an easy-to-use guide for daily actions and thought. Stockdale was able to maintain control while in captivity because he embraced the tenets of Stoic thought.

Stoicism is practical for everyday living and beneficial when you need to make important decisions. Many philosophical schools of thought run parallel, so you might recognize principles of Stoicism in your own religious or philosophical studies. They influenced many philosophers and religious leaders throughout history.

There are things within our power, and there are things beyond our power. Within our power are our opinion, aim, desire, dislikes, and, in summary, whatever is our own. Beyond our power is property, reputation, duties, and, in summary, whatever is not ours.

~Epictetus[16]

---

15   Graver, "Epictetus."
16   Epictetus and James Harris, *Epictetus, The Enchiridion: Adapted for the Contemporary Reader*,7.

According to Epictetus, The Four Pillars of Stoicism are wisdom, temperance, justice, and courage.

Wisdom

Wisdom refers to your ability to determine what you have control over and what you have no control over. Stoic philosophy says you can only control yourself in your thoughts and your actions. Before you act, you must first think. You must ask yourself: Is this action in response to something and does that something matter? Can your actions change anything, and will that change be positive or negative?

In Stockdale's case, his physical freedom was gone. The North Vietnamese Army had massive influence over his movement, his health, and his physical safety. Despite what looked like complete domination, he refused to relinquish control over who he was, his mind, and his response to their actions. I use *influence* to describe his captors' position because of a principle of leadership that demonstrates three things: our sphere of control, our sphere of influence, and outside factors where we have no control and no influence.

Imagine a sphere containing all the things you have no control over and zero influence over. Within that sphere is a smaller sphere containing everything you have influence over but no control. Within that sphere, a smaller sphere containing all of the things you have control over.

The sphere of control contains who you are: your mindset, your values, your logic, your decisions, your emotions, and your actions. Outside of that control but within your sphere of influence are people, events, health, relationships, status, wealth, etc. Outside of that is everything else, where you have no control and no influence.

People have a natural tendency to concern themselves with people, events, weather, and tragedies they have no influence over or control over. However, when you focus attention and energy on the outer circle, you are wasting your energy on things you cannot change. At the same time, you have less energy to dedicate to the inner circles where you can actually make a difference.

The central circle is where you come to your decisions, and how you guide your thoughts. It's where you improve yourself, develop your leadership skills and work on your mindset. These things are under your control, and that is where your energy and focus should be.

The second circle contains your personal and other relationships along with your sphere of influence. As your sphere of influence grows, you'll find you have less concern with things outside that circle where you have no ability to make any changes.

Whenever I experience negative emotions, as a litmus test I ask a couple of questions: Is this something that my emotions, words, or actions can change? If the answer is no, I have zero reason to continue feeling anything but indifference toward it. If the answer is yes, then I ask myself whether I am willing to act towards making a change about this. If the answer is no, indifference is still the answer.

If I'm (1) willing to take action toward change, (2) if that action demonstrates integrity with my core values, and (3) if the outcome is for the greater good, then that event is within my sphere of influence. Only then will I take action. This principle will not only make you a better leader, but it will also give you a much happier life.

This idea frequently comes into play on the job. Everyone has a boss. Let's say for example, your boss takes a harsh stance on some issue and hands down an unpopular directive with instructions that your team members must comply. If they don't, you will have to terminate them.

Whether you agree with the directive or not is immaterial. You have a job to do and that is to deliver this directive to your team and see that each member carries it out. You can approach this a couple of ways. You can let your emotions take over and become upset because you don't agree with the directive or you don't agree with the harsh way it was given. You can pass your negative emotions to your team and watch the situation unravel. Your sphere of influence will contract when your team goes into a negative emotional state. They could decide on an undesirable response, and you won't be able to stop them. You will have to terminate them. Careers will suffer, and families will suffer.

On the other hand, you can notice that the directive is outside of your control and influence. You cannot change it. In that case, you disengage your emotions. You do have control over how you receive that information, how you process it and how you pass it along to your team members. You can put your energy toward getting the best outcome possible for your team.

First, you come up with a strategy on how to positively influence your team, so they see the value of the task at hand. You can omit the threats and ask the team, "Does anyone have any ideas about how to get this done in the most efficient way that will also let us have some fun." By asking for suggestions, you're creating a team environment where you are looking at the issue together and you will get through it together. Your team will also have more respect as you show them that you are able to bring them through difficult situations.

This same principle applies to any dramatic change or tragedy. It's okay to grieve the loss of whatever you might have lost, but then take a look at what is still within your control—your mindset, your attitude, your next action steps, the way you see yourself, and on and on. From that position, you can make the best decisions possible, continue to have a positive influence where you can and let go of your emotional attachment to what you cannot control or influence. Doing this, you will maintain your stability, and your life can continue in a positive direction.

Your influence over the world around you directly correlates to how others view you in the realm of leadership. Great leaders throughout history have studied Stoicism and acted within its principles because they are effective.

Temperance

Temperance encompasses self-control and contentment. When making a decision about whether to take action, ask yourself, "Is this a necessity?" If it isn't, choose to focus your time and energy toward more essential activities. Work on doing them more effectively and better.

Like muscle building, self-control and contentment must be strengthened through thoughtful practice and repetition. Gratitude meditation where you imagine things you are thankful for will help strengthen your sense of contentment. Consider this from Marcus Aurelius: "And as for thy life, consider what it is; a wind; not one constant wind neither, but every moment of an hour let out, and sucked in again."[17] If all you have to be thankful for is your in-breath and your out-breath that keep you alive, be thankful for that. Be thankful for one breath at a time.

Courage

Courage is important when it comes to integrity. Many situations will put you at a crossroads where one action will bring pleasure and a different action will cause you less pleasure or outright pain. Integrity means doing the right thing despite inconvenience, embarrassment, anxiety, hardship, or other unpleasantness. This is where courage comes into play.

Epictetus said, "There are two vices much blacker and more serious than the rest: lack of persistence and lack of self-control

---

17 Marcus Aurelius (Author), Meric Casaubon (Translator), *Meditations*, 28.

… persist and resist."[18] If your efforts are noble and for the greater good, persist. When you fall, when you fail, when discomfort is certain, resist the temptation to take the easy way when it undermines your integrity. Never ignore wrongs when you have the power to make them right. Have the courage to do the right thing even though it causes discomfort. Don't take the easy way out.

Justice

Justice means working for the greater good. This is vital for effective leadership. Selfish-Altruism plays a part in working for justice. As a strong leader, you must actively care for the well-being of others. Strive to be your best, so you are an asset for the team. Your thoughts and actions should be directed toward the common good.

Marcus Aurelius said, "Men exist for the sake of one another. Teach them then or bear with them."[19] You have a responsibility to educate your fellow man to improve their lives. If you shirk that responsibility, you must be willing to accept the shortcomings of those around you when they fail to meet your expectations.

According to Stoic philosophy, a virtuous leader exhibits courageous self-leadership and acts with integrity in order to serve the greater good. The Stoics believed virtue was the only absolute good.

"A virtuous leader exhibits courageous self-leadership and acts with integrity in order to serve the greater good."

---

18   "How to Be a Stoic: an evolving guide to practical Stoicism for the 21st century" HowToBeAStoic.wordpress.com, May 21, 2015, Accessed August 31, 2021.
19   Aurelius, *Meditations*, 133.

Epictetus sought above all to foster ethical development in others, keeping his personal and intellectual satisfaction strictly subordinate.[20] This is a large piece of what leadership is about: ensuring the success of others before concerning yourself with pursuits that benefit you alone. You must develop yourself with the intent to benefit others. In order to do that, you must understand the needs of others, so you can be equipped to contribute to their success. This takes us back to communication, the foundation of effective leadership.

In my own exploration of core values, brainstorming with my daughter was a wonderful exercise. I would encourage you to do the same with your child or someone close to you. This conversation helped us share what we believe are our most important values, not just as a leader but as a person who desires to be their best self and consistently demonstrate that in every choice they make.

During our brainstorming session, my daughter and I narrowed down to four values. We wrote definitions for them and came up with an anchoring statement, something like a slogan or mantra.

1. Wisdom—before taking action, know what you have control over and what you have zero control over
2. Morality—being empathetic, compassionate and ethical
3. Fortitude—perseverance in the face of adversity; being courageous when it is easier and less painful to succumb to your fears
4. Moderation—tempering your words and behavior through self-control

We condensed these four values into this statement: Leadership Through Virtue and Action. I plugged that phrase into

---

20 Graver, "Epictetus."

Google Translate Latin and out came the fanciness: Ductu Per Virtutem Et Actionem. This is what I strive for, not just in word but in deed.

Ductu Per Virtutem Et Actionem:
Leadership Through Virtue and Action

One day, people close to you will write down a few words to read in front of your friends and family about how you touched their lives. You are writing those words in their hearts right now. What will they say?

Action Step 3: Identify your core values.

Below is a list of values pertaining to leadership. You might have others you wish to add. I have provided a few blanks, so you can add those below.

Thinking of leaders you admire, go down the list and find a value they exhibit that you strongly relate to. Compare that word with all the others. If another word beats your first pick, switch to that one as your favorite and keep comparing until you have an all-time favorite. Repeat the process until you have 3 or 4 values that consistently outshine the rest. List those four in the blanks below.

- Justice
- Judgment
- Dependability
- Initiative
- Decisiveness
- Tact
- Integrity

- Enthusiasm
- Bearing
- Unselfish
- Courage
- Knowledge
- Loyalty
- Endurance
- Encouraging
- Trusted
- A good coach
- A good teacher
- Credible
- Listens well
- Persuasive
- Mentoring
- Keeps cool under pressure
- Clearly explains missions, standards and priorities
- Sees the big picture, provides context and perspective
- Can make tough, sound decisions on time
- Adapts quickly to new situations and requirements
- Sets high standards without a "zero defects" mentality
- Can handle "bad news"
- Coaches and gives useful feedback to subordinates
- Sets a high ethical tone, demands honest reporting
- Knows how to delegate and not micromanage
- Builds and supports teamwork within staff and among units
- Is positive, encouraging and realistically optimistic

Your Core values:

1. _____

2. _____

3. _____

4. _____

Put your findings to the test with these two exercises:

1. Think about major decisions or events in your life and see how those values made an impact on your actions.
2. Going back to those few words spoken before your friends and family, are the values on your list included in your eulogy in some form?

CHAPTER 4:

Why Are You Doing This?

Why do great leaders hold true against all odds? What drives them and keeps them going when others quit and go home? Why do the Nelson Mandela's of this world choose to stay in prison when all they have to do is sign the paper and walk out?

In 1985 when Nelson Mandela received the provisional release offer, he hadn't seen his wife, Winnie, for twenty years because she was under house arrest in another part of the country. His four children didn't have their father. Yet, he held on for five more years until he left prison on his own terms.

What drives you to hold on when others walk away? What causes you to quit? Looking back at your life, what prompted you to make the most difficult decisions of your past? The answers touch the tender areas of your life that you might feel hesitant to explore. Even a conversation with a friend or loved one where that person demands, "Why did you do that?" causes immediate tension in your stomach. Your throat closes a little as you try to summon up a response.

The answer to that big question, "Why," is the bottom line of your life, yet it often hides under the surface. Few people have the courage to explore it fully. Strong leaders set themselves apart because they are willing to do the hard work. They strip all excuses from their mind and make a deliberate commitment to follow through, no matter what. Finding the answer to the big question, "Why?" is one of the toughest things you will tackle.

If you wonder whether or not you are capable of this level of commitment, I would say, "Accept the challenge to keep reading." This might be the missing piece to the puzzle for you to reach your full potential. You have a role in this life. You have a purpose. When you understand what drives you, you can achieve so much more, and the world around you will be better because of it.

"When you understand what drives you,
you can achieve so much more."

All pursuits have a layer of personal gratification. When I began studying leadership, I realized I wanted my name to mean something after I was gone. I wanted my legacy to honor the name of my father and my grandfather. That was my external reason why. Other external motivations might be love for country, helping the community or fighting for a cause. Millions of people have made the ultimate sacrifice for these reasons. External motivations are powerful.

Along with positive external motivations, everyone experiences pressures that are not their own. Maybe your mother always told you that you should be a doctor, maybe someone expects you to take over the family business, or possibly your spouse wants you to stay at that job you hate because of the lifestyle it provides. You might love that person and want to please them, so you have a stressful conversation going on in your mind while you feel heavy inside. You tell yourself you're strong enough to get through this. You promise yourself that at some point in the future you'll do what you really want. You expend a tremendous amount of effort at tasks others seem to find easy.

These are signs that you are acting on someone else's motivations, not your own. Outside pressures are a part of life. Everyone has them. The key to strong leadership is to identify the situation, to extricate yourself from living up to someone else's ideals, and focus your energies toward your own vision and goals. You simply cannot fulfill your purpose while hitched to someone else's wagon.

While external motivations are powerful, internal motivations are inevitable. Internal motivations are the driving force inside you, that you may or may not be aware of. These drivers will not be denied. Fortunately, internal motivations can be directed, modified, and managed.

"Internal motivations are inevitable."

Internal motivation is different from core values. My four core values are wisdom, morality, fortitude, and moderation. Why do

I work so hard to hold fast to those values and stay in the game? The answer to that question is my internal motivation. For me, it's my personal obligation to maintain my integrity, my resolution to honor my heritage, and my desire to leave a shining example for my daughter. I want to stay true to myself and make my family proud. That is the root cause of my own version of Selfish-Altruism.

Psychology books contain hundreds of reasons people behave as they do. Here are several that relate to leadership.

Post-Traumatic Stress Disorder (PTSD)

During my time in the fire service, I have seen horrific things. Eventually, they led to a PTSD diagnosis. I knew I was experiencing symptoms of PTSD but rather than seeking help when I first noticed, I pushed through and allowed stress to dominate my life. Stress of that sort has many victims. When stress levels are too high, decision-making abilities are low and personal relationships suffer.

Self-care is vital when leading people in high stress environments. You have a personal responsibility to maintain a healthy lifestyle and have an accurate level of awareness when it comes to how you respond to events around you. Self-awareness is useless if you ignore your obligation to take care of yourself.

PTSD is defined by the American Psychiatric Association (APA) as a psychiatric disorder that can occur in people who have experienced or witnessed a traumatic event such as a natural disaster, a serious accident, a terrorist act, war and combat, rape or other violent personal assault. People with PTSD have intense, disturbing thoughts and feelings related to their experience that last long after the traumatic event has ended. They might re-live the event through flashbacks or nightmares. They might feel sadness, fear or anger, and they might feel detached or estranged from other people. People with PTSD often avoid situations or people that remind them of the traumatic event, and they can have strong negative reactions to something as ordinary as a loud noise or an accidental touch.[21]

A diagnosis of PTSD first depends on exposure to an upsetting traumatic event. Exposure could be indirect as well as firsthand. For example, PTSD could occur in an individual learning about the violent death of a close family member. It can also occur as a result of exposure to horrible details of trauma such as police officers exposed to the facts and photos of child abuse cases.[22]

The APA's website goes on to detail the symptoms of PTSD as follows:

Symptoms of PTSD fall into four categories. Specific symptoms can vary in severity.

1. Intrusive thoughts such as repeated, involuntary memories; distressing dreams; or flashbacks of the traumatic event. Flashbacks may be so vivid that people feel they are re-living the traumatic experience or seeing it before their eyes.

2. Avoiding reminders of the traumatic event may include avoiding people, places, activities, objects and situations that bring on distressing memories. People may try to avoid remembering or thinking about the traumatic event. They may resist talking about what happened or how they feel about it.

---

21 "What Is Posttraumatic Stress Disorder?" American Psychiatric Association, Accessed August 31, 2021.

22 Ibid.

3. Negative thoughts and feelings may include ongoing and distorted beliefs about oneself or others (e.g., "I am bad," "No one can be trusted"); ongoing fear, horror, anger, guilt or shame; much less interest in activities previously enjoyed; or feeling detached or estranged from others.
4. Arousal and reactive symptoms may include being irritable and having angry outbursts; behaving recklessly or in a self-destructive way; being easily startled; or having problems concentrating or sleeping.[23]

Polyvagal theory is the idea that every person needs three physiological states: social engagement, fight or flight, and freeze. These states are attached to your biology and lead to physiological states which affect how you feel and how you behave. Your perception of threat or safety in your environment triggers these three states. This is not a cognitive perception as much as your nervous system's assessment of threat levels around you.[24] It's feeling the hair standing up on your arms, increased heartrate and sudden hyper-sensitivity to sights and sounds. Something inside you knows you are in danger.

In PTSD, a traumatic event has ramped up the sympathetic nervous system to high alert. After the event is past, the body continues in that hyper state, including lingering memories in the back of your mind, flashbacks, and nightmares about the event. Below is a chart from Rubyjowalker.com that explains it more fully.

---

23 Ibid.
24 Ruby Jo Walker, "Polyvagal Theory: informs all the work I do and teach."

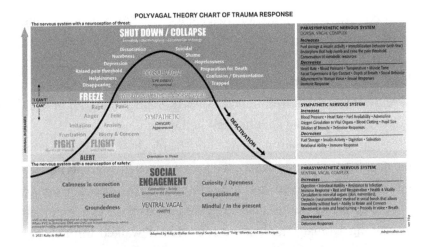

POLYVAGAL THEORY CHART OF TRAUMA RESPONSE

When I began my career, I experienced several traumatic calls early on. Within my first year I watched parents break as we informed them that we couldn't save their baby. I was sometimes the last person someone saw before they died. Shootings, stabbings, traffic accidents, child abuse, animal attacks, structure fires, and construction accidents were part of my job.

Another layer of stress came from being responsible for rescuing people, treating patients and supporting the families of the deceased. When you share a common experience with someone in the throes of grief, you automatically take a plunge into an abyss of emotions that is hard to regulate. You must manage this stress in a healthy way to ensure you remain effective in your role as a leader.

"You must manage this stress in a healthy way to ensure you remain effective in your role as a leader."

Early one morning, I was dispatched to a call where a young mother answered the door of her apartment when her ex-boyfriend knocked. When she opened the door, he shot her in the head, leaned into the apartment and shot the woman's teenage daughter several times. He turned around, walked to the parking lot in front of the apartment, and shot himself in the head.

In spite of gunshot wounds to the head, chest, back, and arm, the daughter survived because the personnel on this call performed masterfully and saved her life. Unfortunately, even a team of trauma surgeons couldn't have repaired the damage to her mother. The dying woman "looked" at me when I walked through her door, and that look will stay with me until I die. Her eyes were fixed, pupils dilated, and aimed right at me. When I leaned down to check for a pulse, her body gasped for air, and she tried hard to communicate to me with her eyes, pleading with me to help her.

My team carried the daughter past on a stretcher, and I watched the girl's heart break as she saw her mother lying in a massive pool of blood on their living room floor. In the moment, I had to stay calm and do my job. Afterwards, I had to sit at my desk and breathe through the flood of emotions coursing through me before I filled out my reports. In the weeks and months that followed I experienced nightmares, sleepless nights, crying for no apparent reason, and mood swings. Drinking became a way for me to limit the unwanted memories of this call and countless others.

Law enforcement personnel, paramedics, EMT's, emergency department personnel, and firefighters all experience trauma as part of the job. Anyone in these professions, and others that experience horrific events, should have frequent trauma support as part of their regular self-care.

Programming and Limiting Beliefs

My mother and father divorced when I was five years old. I remember being so excited I couldn't stand still when my brother, Sean, and I were going to spend the weekend with our dad. When Dad wasn't at the fire station, he worked as a respiratory therapist at a local hospital. Sometimes he ran late due to work-related delays. Our mother would watch us looking out the front window brimming with anticipation of our father's arrival. When he was late, our mother would say, "Well, I guess your father doesn't love us anymore." She would load us up in the station wagon, and we would leave. Even if he arrived five minutes later, we would have no visit with our dad that weekend.

Many hidden programs and limiting beliefs formed in my young mind from those days, such as love is conditional, I am not worthy of love, and the things you value the most might be stripped away at a moment's notice, to name a few. Limiting beliefs had a massive impact on my relationships—both in my career and personal life.

My mother dated men who weren't the highest caliber. I witnessed her endure beatings and verbal abuse, and she behaved violently as well. I recall getting slapped in the face many times until I moved in with my dad when I was twelve.

She was my mother, and I loved her very much, but I have memories of her that I wish I didn't have. She was a nurse and had frequent migraines. One of the doctors she worked for gave her injections of Demerol and Phenergan to help the pain. As time went on, she became dependent on opiates and ended up permanently disabled. She spent most days lying in bed or on the couch. She attempted suicide multiple times. Many times, I found her unconscious on the floor from an "accidental" overdose.

She passed away a few years ago. I was the next of kin who lived closest, so I had to drive to her house, meet with law enforcement and identify her body. My only comfort is that she and I had begun repairing our relationship and had planned to see each other later that week. Our last conversation ended with both of us saying, "I love you."

I carried a lot of anger knowing that my mother became an addict because doctors gave her narcotics. If not dealt with, that kind of simmering anger can sabotage many other areas of your life.

"Simmering anger can sabotage many other areas of your life."

Several years before Mom died, my brother, Sean, and I became very close in 2005. At some point in 2006 or 2007 he became depressed and got involved with crack cocaine. On Christmas Day, 2009, Sean and I had a falling out. Before we repaired our relationship, he died on February 4, 2010.

Two years before his death, Sean had entered a drug treatment facility and got clean. When he was discharged, he came home with me. I gave him a job in my small company, installing rain gutters with me on my days off from the fire department. He did great for a while, but after he moved in with his new girlfriend, he started using again, this time with pain killers.

Eventually, he and his girlfriend moved in with my mother where his son, Aiden, was born. Sean cleaned up again. Then, he tried to break up a dog fight and got a bad bite in his calf muscle. He told the hospital that he was an addict and couldn't take pain medication. They gave him an anti-inflammatory instead. Unfortunately, infection set in, and the wounds became necrotic. This time, he had no choice but to take strong painkillers. Once his leg healed, he began methadone treatment.

One night, he and his girlfriend had an argument, and she left. My mom gave Sean a Valium and told him to lie down and relax. The combination of methadone and Valium shut down his respiratory drive. He suffocated in his sleep.

I received a phone call from a friend of mine, a lieutenant at the fire station down the street from my mother's house. He told me that my brother was found unresponsive that morning, and there wasn't anything they could do. I called my father, and all I could say was, "Sean's dead." I heard his soul break before the phone disconnected.

I kissed my wife and daughter goodbye and drove to my mom's house. On the way, I remember crying uncontrollably, punching the steering wheel, ceiling, and dash of my truck as I yelled obscenities while driving down the shoulder of the interstate. When I arrived, my mother and Sean's girlfriend were on the front porch smoking cigarettes. I asked where Aiden, my nephew, was and went to his room.

My brother's door was open, and two deputies were just inside his doorway. I could see his body, his head, and his very hairy leg (he had notoriously hairy legs). I went into the baby's room and changed Aiden's diaper, then took him outside. Later, my dad and I were invited inside the house by the medical examiner to say our goodbyes before they took Sean away.

I went in and kissed him on his freshly shaved head. I told him that I loved him, hugged him and looked at him one last time with my hand on his head. I blacked out. I next became aware of my surroundings as my dad put his hand on my shoulder. I had ripped the gate from the chain link fence between my mom's house and the neighbor's. I had smashed it against the ground, punching the ground and yanking out clods of grass while emitting some type of guttural cry. I changed in a very dark way that day.

The next month was our sixth wedding anniversary, so my wife and I went to the beach with our daughter for a few days. I awoke early one morning and went for a run on the beach to clear my head. I ran north as fast as I could, like I was trying to outrun the pain of losing my brother. I ran so far that I had to sprawl on the sand, too exhausted to run back, in agony because I couldn't outrun the pain.

I lay there, looking at the ocean and thinking that I could swim out and bury myself at sea. When I stood up, I realized I didn't have enough energy to get deep enough to make the effort count. That day wasn't my day to go. As I trudged back, I became angry with myself for wanting to give up. I had more left to do, even if it was just to give my family a good life.

As I walked down the beach, I looked at all the beautiful homes with views of the Atlantic. I imagined myself doing something valuable enough that I could one day enjoy those same views. At that moment, I remembered baby Aiden, who would never know his father. Before the addiction, Sean was an amazing man. He was smarter than me, funnier than me, kinder than me, and far more deserving of the joy life has to offer.

I made it my mission to live my life in a way that I could mentor Aiden and explain to him the value of helping others. I would tell him about some of my achievements and that I'm only a fraction of what his father was. His father would have helped so many more than I have. We are blood. He is his father's son. He has greatness in his blood. That day, I gave myself a purpose and a goal. I made myself strong.

The next few years were a learning and growing phase for me. During this time, Aiden, and his younger half-brother, Tristen, were taken from their mother by social services in Virginia. Ultimately, I gained custody of Aiden and Tristen for a year. Their maternal grandmother asked the court in Virginia for custody of the boys. Because she was blood related to both brothers, and I was only related to Aiden, the judge felt she was the appropriate relative to raise them. This was a heavy blow.

Shortly after that, my marriage deteriorated at an alarming rate. It had been strained, but now it was failing. Marriage counseling was not effective, and we divorced when my daughter was nine years old. Ironically, the divorce was finalized on the sixth anniversary of my brother's death.

I was passed over for my next promotion, and I allowed my judgment to slide. I was in so much emotional pain that I wanted more than anything to feel better. I dated a close friend's ex-girlfriend and ended that friendship, as well as creating a strain on many other personal and professional relationships. After living with this woman for a while, our relationship ended. Broken relationships, hurt friends, and a sketchy reputation with my colleagues—my poor choices were coming from trauma-based motivations. I had hidden programs running my life, and I didn't realize it. I needed outside input, but I didn't go for help.

I was looking for affection to fill the dark void inside me. No other person can fill that void. I know that now. I had a negative internal program running my choices based on pain, grief and unresolved anger.

Where are your motivations coming from? Are you reacting to trauma and unresolved grief? Are you in pain, enduring a constant state of fight/flight or freeze? Or is your internal drive related to a healthy resolve to maintain your integrity and leave the world a better place?

I cannot stress enough the importance of getting help resolving the negative drives in your life and to make sure you are working from positive motivations. Introspection is one way to take stock. Another way is to observe your past behavior. Are you making decisions based on wanting to feel better? Are you reacting out of trauma triggers that leave you with less-than-optimum results?

When you run into a series of roadblocks or "bad luck," that's the time to pause and check in. You might have negative internal motivations you aren't aware of. Many experiences you have endured aren't your fault. They are simply part of the human experience, and you can't control that. What you can control is your own thinking and behaviors. That means accessing help to get through it.

"When you run into a series of roadblocks or "bad luck,"
that's the time to pause and check in."

As a leader with questionable internal motivations, you will struggle to lift others higher than yourself, so be diligent in practicing self-care. In turn, you will amplify your influence and inspire more people to follow you.

When Nelson Mandela first raised his face to the sun as a free man, he had a spark inside him that everyone could see. A few years later, he became President of South Africa. If he had allowed bitterness and anger to overcome him, he would have never fulfilled his purpose, and neither will you.

Action Step 4: Identify your primary motivations.

1. What drives you? When your back is against the wall, what keeps you going?

   _____

   _____

   _____

   _____

2. List your two primary external motivations.

   a. _____

   _____

   b. _____

   _____

3. List your two primary internal motivations.

   a. _____

   _____

   b. _____

   _____

4. Are any of these motivations coming from someone else's values or desires?

   _____

   _____

   _____

   _____

CHAPTER 5:

What's In Your Way?

Every goal or project comes with obstacles. When you build a house, you check the property for underground springs, boulders, and mature trees with massive root systems, so you can make plans for those when you put in the foundation. You check local building codes and verify supply lines. You plan for as many obstacles as possible before you break ground, so you can begin with an idea of the cost and create a timeline for the work.

Each step of the project comes with its own obstacles. The same is true for your Grand Strategy.

Your Own Thinking

One of the biggest obstacles you will ever face is your own thinking. Daniel Goleman is known internationally for his work as a psychologist, an author, researcher and lecturer.[25] He is an expert on emotional intelligence and the role it plays in personal and professional excellence. Two of his books were required reading when I completed my Master's Degree in Public Administration: Primal Leadership and Emotional Intelligence.

Emotional Intelligence

In Goleman's research, he found four domains of emotional intelligence: self-awareness, self-management, social awareness, and relationship management. These all come into play when you create your Grand Strategy. Self-awareness is linked to self-control or self-management, which every effective leader strives for. Social awareness is the ability to empathize with others.

When you are aware of how you respond, you have more control over your emotional outbursts and any visual cues that others might see as negativity. If you can give a measured response even during strong emotions, others will see you as someone who is in control. When your reptilian brain heads toward fight/flight or freeze, you want your higher brain to moderate any actions that aren't consistent with your values.

Empathizing with others gives you the ability to better understand what they are saying and what they are not saying. It also heightens your self-awareness, so you can understand how others receive your behavior and your words. Self-management, self-awareness, and social awareness are all important in managing relationships and building trust, the core of effective leadership. However, empathy should not be mistaken for weakness. Empathetic leadership fosters willingness in people because they know their leader will always look out for them.

---

25 "About Daniel Goleman," DanielGoleman.info.

Assumptions

Another obstacle created by your own thinking is assumptions. This is a tricky area because the nature of assumptions makes them difficult to spot. Assumptions happen in the moment, and they fly under the radar.

A few years ago, I was working as the Battalion Chief in an area hit hard by thunderstorms. The storm caused many false alarms. Around 9 p.m. one of my engine crews was dispatched to an apartment complex because a resident had called 911 for assistance with her Wi-Fi box.

She said her box made a noise and started smoking. It was no longer smoking but had a lingering odor. She was worried about safety. The 911 operator dispatched the closest engine company for a non-emergency call. The engine company had been going from false alarm to false alarm for the past four hours and had little reason to suspect that this was any different.

When I began listening to the call, I headed in that direction in case I was needed. I heard additional units being dispatched. When Engine 63 arrived, an orange glow was coming from the roof of the three-story apartment building. Lightening had struck the building, and the attic was on fire. The fire engine arrived in front of the building while residents stared out their windows, unaware the building was burning.

The lieutenant called for appropriate resources, directed crews to evacuate the building, and began deploying hoselines and equipment for a rapid attack on the fire. The chief running the neighboring battalion was closer to the call than I was, so he was dispatched.

When I arrived, I was assigned as Division 3, the officer in charge of operations on the third floor. By this point, several hoselines had been deployed. The first ladder company on scene was prepared to flow water from the elevated master stream mounted on the top of their 75-foot turntable ladder. Due to a malfunction with Engine 63, water had yet to be applied to the fire.

By this time, Engine 63's Lieutenant (E63 LT) was on the third floor with multiple personnel, trying to gain access to the attic for quick extinguishment. Without functioning hoselines, the fire was burning freely and had vented itself through the roof. Fire was also coming from the gabled end of the roof.

I took position on the third floor. I tried to contact the E63 LT on the radio to get a status report, but I couldn't make myself heard through heavy radio traffic. I had no information about current conditions, actions underway, or resources they needed (other than what I could see through the smoke).

I heard the lieutenant from the ladder company (Quint 67/Q67 LT) advising that they were prepared to flow the master stream and asking Command if he should flow water. Before I could get a status update, Command asked me if we were ready for water.

This meant 600 to 1200 gallons of water per minute flowing at 80 to 100 psi. A lightweight truss roof will collapse under this much pressure, especially after exposure to fire conditions. Protocol requires any personnel near the target area to clear out before an elevated master stream begins to flow water. The fire had already compromised the structural integrity of the truss system, so the apartment roof was already undermined. Any people under that part of the roof were in danger of injury or death.

E63 LT on the third floor was focused on getting water to the fire. He had repeatedly requested the hoselines to be charged. When he heard Command asking if we were ready for water, he said yes and told them to flow water. Still unable to communicate over heavy radio traffic, I was aware of what was about to happen. I immediately directed the crews operating under the burning attic space to go down to the second floor. I then saw E63 LT and made contact. I told him they were about to flow the master stream.

The big water started flowing.

Fearing for his people's safety, the lieutenant grabbed the two firefighters near him. The three of them made their way toward the back of the building through the breezeway to ensure that the other crews working in the third-floor apartments at the back moved to a safe location on the second floor.

The stream of water moved in our direction toward the seat of the fire. The roof collapsed.

Everything went black and then had an orange glow. The lieutenant was no longer where I had last seen him halfway down the breezeway. I feared the worst. When the roof collapsed, radio traffic ceased. Now that I was able to speak on the radio, I directed the truck company to flow water over the breezeway.

When it had cooled enough, I directed them back toward the area over the apartments. I headed through the breezeway but saw no sign of the lieutenant or anyone else and went down the stairs to the second floor. Everyone was safe. With the fire knocked down and the hoselines functioning, we soon finished the job.

We faced several obstacles during this event where our primary goals were (1) the safety and wellbeing of the residents, (2) the reasonable safety and wellbeing of all firefighters on scene and (3) putting out the fire. The most obvious obstacles were the communication breakdown and equipment malfunction, but just as important were the assumptions.

As I've stated before, communication is one of the pivotal skills for an effective leader. Too often, obstacles arise because of broken or flawed communication. In this case, lives were in jeopardy.

> *"Communication is one of the pivotal skills*
> *for an effective leader."*

The Wildland Fire Service in the United States uses the five communication responsibilities to ensure effective communication within their ranks. As a leader, you must stay informed. You must also ensure that both those you lead and those you follow are informed. This is true for any team, anywhere, from a corporate boardroom to a tugboat crew.

Here are the Five Communications Responsibilities given by the Wildland Fire Service:

Brief—use briefings to ensure accurate situation awareness.

Debrief—use After Action Reviews to build accountability and learn from experience.

Acknowledge and understand messages—acknowledge and ensure you are clear about received communications on conditions, assigned tasks, intent, and other important information.

Communicate hazards to others—use hazard identification, a key component of risk management, to identify personal, tactical, situational, political, or organizational hazards. Good leaders ensure that team members are vigilant for hazards and communicate identified hazards effectively.

Ask if you don't know—guard against making false assumptions when the picture is not clear.[26] [Emphasis mine.]

Gathering information quickly and effectively is fundamental to successful leadership. This means developing the ability to ask questions that result in succinct-yet-complete answers. Open ended questions help, but you must be willing to give the other person enough time to reply while you listen attentively. Of course, in emergency situations like the apartment fire, time is of the essence, so the expected reply is either a confirmation or a request for clarification.

For example, directing a crew that you want them to evacuate the third floor of a building, you would say to the crew, "I need you to go to the third floor and evacuate everybody off the third floor down the back stairwell to the rear of the building."

Their response should be, "Understood. We are heading to the third floor to evacuate everyone down the back stairwell to the rear of the structure," or, "Understood. Evacuating the third floor, but what was the last part?" The listener either repeats the directive or asks a clarifying question. Otherwise, you risk dangerous miscommunication, as in the case here. Misunderstood directives result in wasted resources, destroyed careers, injuries or loss of life. Thankfully, the men and women involved in the apartment fire had established relationships that allowed for quick action even in the face of communication failures.

When facing obstacles, clarity in your thinking is an absolute necessity in order to see the matter resolved.

---

26 "Five Communication Responsibilities," National Wildfire Coordinating Group.

Other People's Thinking

Another obstacle to reaching your goal is other people's thinking. Effective leaders manage their own sphere of control, and they manage their relationships with the people inside their sphere of influence. The only real measure of your success as a leader is the success of your team. You can't ensure your team's success if you don't know them.

Engage other people. Listen twice as much as you talk. Sometimes people are guarded and need encouragement to open up. Use their name, smile, ask open-ended questions about their interests and their personal lives and professional goals. Make sure your interest in others is genuine. Let them know their success is important to you.

Avoid disagreement when an opinion differs from yours. If someone's opinions have a negative effect on the team, first understand what led them to form those opinions. Respecting their ideas and desires will help you appeal to a more virtuous rationale. Challenge them to become more of a leader and offer them guidance.

Follow through with your commitments. Be authentic in your positive valuation, and avoid disapproval or judgment. Give people something to live up to.

"Give people something to live up to."

One of the first books I read on leadership was entitled *It's Your Ship* by Captain D. Michael Abrashoff. Captain Abrashoff would bring each sailor into his office and speak with them about their goals and desires. He asked them personal questions and got to know them. He also set goals for his personnel and valued their feedback.

One of Abrashoff's methods included charging each sailor with learning the job of the person above them and teaching their job to the people below them. This method creates a sense of pride and evokes a feeling of value. It fosters teamwork. The education of subordinates enhances the skill level of those doing the educating. Learning the job of the person above you not only prepares you for the future, but helps you know what is required of that position, so you can foresee the needs of your boss and eliminate many obstacles before they happen.

Your team members' emotions drive their successes and failures. People want to experience achievement and be recognized for it. Think about how powerful emotions are, and the role they play in your life.

You can recall all of your best and worst memories in detail. Your body chemistry changes during those moments, beginning with the amygdala, the primal brain. Sometimes referred to as the reptilian brain, the amygdala drives your automatic self-preservation behaviors known as the 4 F's: feeding, fighting, fleeing, and family building (reproduction). It plays the primary role in processing memory, emotional responses, and can influence decision-making.

When you influence a person's emotions, you activate the amygdala and influence their decision making. If you are able to create positive emotions within your people, you can inspire them toward enthusiastic performance and mission success. Help your team build actionable memories by engaging the amygdala through creating stress during the exercise, followed by praise when the team meets expectations. This type of influence puts the team into forward momentum and mitigates pushback when tasks get tough.

---

*"This type of influence puts the team
into forward momentum and mitigates pushback
when tasks get tough."*

Self-awareness and mastery of your emotions require thoughtful practice. Regardless of the situation, a leader must be able to take a positive approach and see every event as an opportunity for success. In some instances, success looks very different from what you originally envisioned.

An ancient Zen proverb tells of a king who placed a large boulder in the middle of the main road leading into the kingdom, blocking the path. He hid in the trees to see how his subjects responded to this massive obstacle. First, a group of wealthy merchants saw the boulder and complained about having to find a different route. Others came close, then turned around.

Eventually, a farmer approached with a load of vegetables he wanted to sell inside the kingdom. He tried to move the boulder with all of his strength, but it wouldn't move. He decided to use some large branches from the woods along the road. Using leverage, he was finally able to roll the boulder and clear the path. Where the boulder had been, he noticed an ornate box in a hole. Inside the box, he found a small fortune and a note from the king thanking whoever successfully overcame the obstacle.

When situations arise that block your efforts and seem to indicate certain failure, as a strong leader you must look for opportunities that will improve the circumstances. If you can't find an opportunity, you must create one.

Sometimes an obstacle is an opportunity to learn what not to do in the future. These lessons can be much more valuable than reaching your original goal. Use them to your advantage. Taking this attitude will help you remain positive when the situation is less than desirable. When you are a leader, your people watch to see how you respond. You can create an environment that promotes positivity and growth or one that promotes negativity and decay. If you allow negativity to take hold, you diminish your ability to lead effectively.

"If you allow negativity to take hold, you diminish your ability to lead effectively."

A few years ago, a major accident took place in central Florida. Multiple vehicles were involved, so there were multiple trauma patients. To complicate matters, two of the vehicles hung precariously over an embankment that led to a very deep retention pond.

The two vehicles—a car and a passenger van—were hooked together via tangled metal. The car had hung up on the guardrail with its rear bumper facing the road and its front bumper angled down toward the retention pond. The van was opposite with its front bumper facing the road and its rear aiming down toward the retention pond. The driver of the car had gone through the windshield and was lying down the embankment. He was the first patient transported from the scene.

Inside the van, several passengers needed to be transported for injuries ranging from moderate to life threatening. One of the van's passengers, a young man, lay at the bottom of the embankment with severe trauma to his head and face that made it clear he was deceased.

Many resources were called in. Along with local law enforcement, EMT, and fire department support, we had a special operations unit that specializes in technical rescue. We also had many ambulances and a helicopter that landed in the roadway.

I was the incident commander on the scene. Crews efficiently cared for the patients and saw them transported out to hospitals. This was a massive undertaking with an active technical rescue in play, support vehicles moving through the area, and a crowd of frantic family members gathering nearby.

About halfway into the call, the shift commander arrived and launched into a barrage of questions when my attention was required elsewhere. This was frustrating, but I stayed focused and ignored as much of his interruption as I could while trying to be respectful. Lives were at stake.

After the last patient was safely in a transport unit, the shift commander gathered the ranking officers together to perform a critique in a condescending tone heavily sprinkled with profanity. Anger hardened the faces of the officers who endured his criticism. He, then, focused his words toward me. Careful to keep my facial expressions clear, I responded in a professional, succinct, and descriptive way, citing the logic I had used for my direction.

When I finished, he didn't have anything more to say and chose to leave the scene. As he walked away, we heard more profanity from him.

This interaction with a superior created anger and doubt in the personnel. I could see them questioning their own actions. The air of negativity was palpable. The debrief could have and should have gone much differently, but since the stage was set, my job was to play my role well. I gathered the personnel still on scene. We took turns discussing what went well and where we need improvement.

I praised the efforts of everyone who made the operation successful. Success in this instance referred to the fact that every viable patient was cared for and transported to the appropriate hospital as quickly as possible. None of our personnel were injured in the operation, another success.

As a group, we identified ways to ensure a higher level of excellence the next time we had a similar situation. These lessons were possible because of open and honest communication with everyone involved. In high stress environments, decisions happen rapidly with incomplete information and multiple variables. The key to success is maintaining awareness of the changing environment and adjusting efforts as needed.

Was the shift commander wrong in how he communicated with the officers on scene? I will admit it could have been handled much differently. However, I can't concern myself with his actions, only mine. I have no control over him or anyone else. However, possibly I could have influenced his actions, and I didn't—at least not in a positive way. My ignoring him could have been the root of his frustration and that led to his behavior toward the entire group. I can't say for sure.

I saw that unpleasant scenario as my failure, not his. In my self-assessment, I determined to spend more effort communicating with my superiors. I decided that whenever I was the ranking chief officer on scene, after an operation was demobilized and before the group's After-Action Review (AAR)—I would have a conversation with my superior to inform them of the efforts we made and the outcomes. I'd ask for their input on items they would like me to address in the AAR and for their perspective on team performance. If they identified actions that reflected poor performance, I'd take responsibility for my own actions, for the performance of my crews, and vow to ensure correction. If I had done this that night, the shift commander would have saved face, and my people would have never experienced the emotions linked to being belittled.

Before you can become an effective leader, you must understand the value of being a good follower. Aristotle said, "He who has never learned to obey cannot be a good commander."[27] The best leaders pay their dues through years of consistency and continuous improvement and that includes good Followership. Anyone can give orders, but leaders show the way by example.

"Before you can become an effective leader, you must understand the value of being a good follower."

Negative Attitudes and Prejudices

People have their own ideas about how the world works, including you and me. When working in team environments, differences in perspective will show up. Some people have a chip on their shoulder. Others want to show superiority through snide remarks or playing demeaning pranks. Any form of disrespect or prejudice creates a wall and limits the optimum effectiveness of a team because a portion of your most important asset—people—is restricted and might even be eliminated, if that person has had enough and decides to leave.

I ran into this in the area of gender diversity in the fire service. When I began training in the fire academy, two women were in my class. I watched them struggle and underperform. Both of them did graduate and became certified firefighters. I heard academy instructors talk about how women have ruined the fire department, including the cliché that the proper term for a firefighter is fire*man*.

---

27 GoodReads.com, "Aristotle."

The fire service is one of several occupations with far fewer women than men. According to 2010 data, cultural bias is responsible for the fact that only about 4.8% of all firefighters are women,[28] one of the lowest of all male-dominated fields.[29] Economists, sociologists, and psychologists have done many studies to discover why, especially in the areas of discrimination, physiology and desire. Many fire service leaders say that discrimination is not an issue. They claim that women don't want to join the fire service because it's dirty and dangerous, and that women also have weaker physiology and can't meet the requirements.

I'm ashamed to say that, at first, I allowed my ignorance to shape my attitude on the topic. That is, until I worked with some women who were as tough as most men and more capable than many. Over time, my perspective on this changed.

In the fire service, women face tremendous resistance from male team members. Some years ago, I heard about an excellent female firefighter who loved the fire service and did her job well. She was sexually assaulted by a superior, a respected leader in the department. When she reported the crime, instead of gaining support from the department, many members launched into full-on harassment, threatening phone calls, and simply making her life miserable. Eventually, she transferred out of that station to an outlying area of the county. The investigation found her superior to be untruthful and likely responsible for attempted rape. In spite of all the evidence, he was not disciplined and was allowed to retire with his full pension.

Blaming the victim is nothing new. We've all heard of cases like this in male-dominated fields, such as the military. Sad to say,

---

28 David R. Hollenbach III, "Women in the Fire Service: A Diverse Culture Leads to a Successful Culture."

29 Denise M. Hulett, et al., *Enhancing Women's Inclusion in Firefighting in the USA.*

this still takes place in the 21st century. Women who do their job with excellence and integrity end up leaving because the cost is too high for them to stay. Others remain in their career but, often, in diminished capacity because of negative pressures around them. What a waste of the most valuable asset to any organization: human potential.

Daniel Goleman's studies show that the most effective leadership style is transformational leadership. Transformational leaders have a high level of emotional intelligence (EI). Other studies show that women have higher EI competencies than men, including self-awareness, self-management, social awareness and managing relationships. Cultural bias effectively eliminates the very leaders who would help advance the organization. The same is true for any bias, such as religion, race and sexual orientation.

As for the assertion that women are weaker and can't make the grade, Fire Departments can increase female success by offering mentoring programs. The Milwaukee Fire Department trains recruits for fourteen weeks prior to the physical agility test. They found that females' strength increased an average of 21% and fitness by 29%. By the end of training, the females' combined size, strength and fitness averaged 96% of their male counterparts.[30] Teamwork training is also effective for both small women and small men.

If the culture became more inclusive, more women might view the fire service as an occupation they could thrive in. Greater numbers of women in the fire service would lead to greater levels of creativity, diversity of ideas, and a superior mechanism for innovation.

---

30   Ibid.

Other people's opinions do have an impact, but you have a choice in your response. When you define yourself, no one else can define you.

"When you define yourself, no one else can define you."

Every situation comes with its own obstacles—from a boulder in the road to flawed communication to archaic organizational culture and personal prejudices. Every obstacle has a reset point to resolve it, remove it, or go around it. The answers are not linear. They are organic and can come from many directions. A leader sees an obstacle as an opportunity to turn the situation into an advantage, always remembering that a valuable lesson is just ahead.

Action Step 5: Get clear on your obstacles.

As you create your Grand Strategy, will you resolve your obstacles, remove them or go around them? List them below.

- _____
  _____
- _____
  _____
- _____
  _____
- _____
  _____
- _____
  _____

- _____
  _____
- _____
  _____

CHAPTER 6:

What Do You Need?

S elf-leadership is the most challenging part of being a strong leader because pride, ego and desire are always ready to get in your way. I know from experience that actions rooted in these three things have effects that might not be immediate, but they will show up at the worst possible time. Self-leadership is the only thing that will keep you walking in your integrity. Without self-leadership, you will surely drift. Pride, ego and desire don't sleep.

"A leader of one may one day lead many, but if you can't lead one, you'll never lead any."
~**Frank Viscuso**, author of *Step Up and Lead*

As you become a better leader, people will speak highly of you. They will seek you out for advice and want to be around you. This is a slippery slope that can lead you into thinking too highly of yourself. Self-confidence is good, but pride is dangerous. Pride can lead to an inflated ego that you can't sustain. When your ego gets ahead of your capabilities, something or someone will come along to put you in your place. Mature leaders know this and keep some level of humility.

Your actions tell the world who you are. If you fail as a self-leader, before long those you lead will become more reserved with their trust and respect for you. Nothing you say will overcome actions that contradict your words. While failure in self-leadership is hard to recover from, sometimes failing is the only way to learn your most important lessons. Failures are inevitable. When that time comes, prepare yourself to do the hard work. Be quick to take ownership and even quicker to start mending the damage.

"Employ your time in improving yourself by other men's writings so that you shall gain easily what others have labored hard for."
~Socrates

Knowing that you will fail and make mistakes gives you awareness that others will also fail and make mistakes. I firmly believe that mistakes come from a place of ignorance—the absence of knowledge or truth. You don't wake up in the morning with the desire to make mistakes. Neither does anyone else. Part of your responsibility as a leader is to limit those mistakes and their severity by reducing ignorance in yourself and your team. Give your team the tools they need ahead of time. When they are clear in their objectives, their impulses will have less chance of overcoming their resolve. Arm yourself with the same advantage.

"When you are clear in your objectives, your impulses will have less chance of overcoming your resolve."

Start at your End State and work backwards to where you are now. Do this in various areas of your life, such as career, health, finances and relationships, to name a few. As you work backwards through each area, you will see common threads. You might see the need for better communication skills in both your career and your personal relationships. Maybe you need to take steps to improve your health which will, in turn, improve your finances as you can increase your productivity. Better health will also improve your relationships. Your life is a web of interconnected parts. As you advance in one area, other areas will be positively affected.

As you look at your Grand Strategy—your action plan to get from where you are to where you want to be—you will notice gaps. Your action plan is a list of steps to bridge those gaps. This includes two areas: what to add and what to subtract.

What to Add

Every step in your journey to your End State comes with its own requirements. What do you need to add to meet those requirements? If you want to be a pilot, you might need more flight hours. If you want to move up through the ranks, you might need more education or more certifications.

On a more personal level, your environment might need some additions. If you want to be a fulltime stock trader, maybe you need a better computer system with multiple monitors and a quiet place to focus. Maybe you need to develop relationships that support you in reaching your goals, such as working out with a friend to keep yourself motivated as you form new habits.

Learning

Every stage of advancement comes with its own learning curve. While researching different philosophies, I came across a method for limiting ignorance outlined in an ancient document about rules of reason, logic, epistemology[31] and metaphysics.[32] You will have a better grasp of the world around you when you have correct knowledge in sixteen categories:

- means of right knowledge: a way to find the truth
- the object of right knowledge: getting to the truth
- doubt: realizing which parts aren't on solid footing
- purpose: knowing why you want the information
- familiar instance: information that you work with on a regular basis
- established tenet: ground rules that have been around for a long time
- members of an inference: certain facts that aid in reasoning
- reasoning: coming to valid conclusions
- ascertainment or results: solution to your questioning
- discussion: sharing information with others
- plausible but misleading debates: topics and questions that go off on a tangent

---

31 The study of the nature of knowledge, justification and the rationality of belief
32 The branch of philosophy that examines the fundamental nature of reality, including the relationship between mind and matter, between substance and attribute, and between potentiality and actuality

- arguing or protesting about unimportant details: focusing on what doesn't matter
- fallacies: assumptions that are not true
- disagreements: discussions where two people can't come to a consensus
- futile reposits: wisecracks and comebacks that have no benefit
- methods of losing an argument[33]: how you approach a discussion where no one will give way

---

"Every stage of advancement comes with
its own learning curve."

In her book, *Perspectives of Reality*, Jeaneane Fowler states that knowledge is not self-revealing. You must make an effort to gain knowledge in a systematic process where you learn correct knowledge and abandon incorrect knowledge.[34] The *Nyaya Sutras* gives four methods for gaining valid knowledge: Perception, Inference, Comparison and Reliable Testimony.[35]

Perception is the primary means of gaining true knowledge. It is sensory awareness, including how you regard, understand, or interpret what you sense. All other epistemic methods are directly

---

33 Hiriyanna, M, *Outlines of Indian Philosophy*, 245,245n.
34 Stephen Phillips, *Epistemology in Classical India: The Knowledge Sources of the Nyaya School.*
35 Karl Potter, T*he Encyclopedia of Indian Philosophies: Indian metaphysics and epistemology*, Vol 2, 222–238.

or indirectly based on perception.[36] You have to become aware of something before you can address it.

"You have to become aware of something
before you can address it."

Inference is knowledge based on perception. It has three forms:

- a priori: using knowledge or experience you already have in order to make a judgment or decision in real time, such as establishing a plan of action for extricating, treating and transporting trauma patients after a multiple-car accident.
- a posteriori: using knowledge, evidence, or experience to make a judgment or decision about something that has already happened, such as a criminal trial.
- commonly seen: a collective understanding, something the group agrees on and holds to, such as supporting the widows of fallen heroes.[37]

Comparison is gaining knowledge based on similarity, comparison, or analogy. It combines hypothesis, examples and tests to understand something new based on what one already knows.[38] This method is especially appropriate for questioning your own beliefs or uncovering the biased opinions of others. Opinions are not facts.

---

36   Jeaneane Fowler, *Perspectives of Reality: An Introduction to the Philosophy of Hinduism*, 134-138.
37   SC Vidyabhushan & NL Sinha (1990), *The Nyâya Sûtras of Gotama*, 4.
38   S Dasgupta, *A History of Indian Philosophy*, Vol 1, 354–360.

Reliable Testimony is asking an expert. This could be a mentor, someone with more skills and experience within your organization, or an outside consultant.

Plato quotes Socrates as stating, "I neither know nor think that I know." This is the Socratic paradox. Plato said Socrates seemed wiser than anyone else because what he didn't know, he didn't think that he knew.[39] Socrates knew that assumptions and jumping to conclusions led to poor judgment and mistakes.

As a leader, you must act with integrity and practice intelligent self-leadership. To accomplish this, you must have accurate self-awareness and eliminate as much ignorance from your thought process as possible. You must seek perfection.

> *"Perfection is not attainable, but if we chase perfection, we can catch excellence."*
> **~Vince Lombardi**

Achievement

Reaching milestones and meeting requirements are part of your Grand Strategy. These are goals that bring you closer to your End State, such as qualifying for a promotion or passing the examination phase in front of a state licensure board. Anyone who wants to become a medical doctor must maintain a 4.0 GPA, so that would go on their list of achievements.

Experience

Experience involves putting in hours. It also means putting yourself in places where you have access to those experiences. Someone who wants to become a golf pro will often work as a

---

39 Plato, *Apology* 21d.

caddie, so they can watch the techniques of others and practice between serving the guests.

Firefighters assigned to a slow station running two calls per shift won't have as much experience as someone working at a busier station running twenty-five calls a shift. Gaining experience involves discipline and motivation. Instead of thinking, "I'm glad my station is slow because I can kick back," someone with a Grand Strategy will say, "I'm not getting enough experience here. I need to be in a place that sees more action."

Another important aspect of experience is training outside your organization to get new perspectives. For example, conventions and conferences for the fire service (such as the FDIC in Indianapolis) where they offer hands-on training [HOT], so attendees get exposure to tactics that might not be in line with their department's standard operating procedures. In my experience, those types of training events exposed me to tactics from across the country that might not apply to my municipality in Florida, where we generally have lightweight trusses and floor joists. Heavier construction types in the Northeast or Midwest lend themselves to more aggressive tactics. A wider range of exposure to various methods is important. When you find yourself in a situation that isn't typical, you'll have that Rolodex slide to refer to, so you can make more informed decisions.

Relationships

Every career or vocation is a people business. Relationships are your most valuable commodity. Whether you're at a tavern or in a conference room, sitting together with team members after a tough assignment means far more than simply blowing off steam. Those times build meaningful relationships, and relationships open doors that no amount of knocking will do. That's also why it's so important to treat people with respect and consideration. The new firefighter at the station could end up being your boss ten years from now. You just never know.

To build better relationships, work on your communication skills. I went through this at length in Chapter 2. Without good communication skills, your journey will be difficult, and you might not reach your desired destination at all.

"Without good communication skills, your journey will be difficult and you might not reach your desired destination."

As you work with others, your dedication to consistency and integrity will lead to growing trust and respect in your own team and beyond. Your sphere of influence will expand. Seek relationships where you can share your knowledge and experience. Teach a seminar. Mentor someone new to your department. Show up in your community.

At the same time, seek relationships that challenge you and help you grow. While you are working on your own learning, achievements and experience, find others who have already been where you are and absorb as much as you can from them. Sometimes, look outside your own field of expertise. For example, whether you want to become an entrepreneur or not, business mentoring can help you with organization and management skills. Stretch your thinking. You cannot expand into your End State by coasting in your comfort zone.

*"You cannot expand into your End State
by coasting in your comfort zone."*

Finding a mentor should be on your list of action steps. Typically, a mentor is someone who is well respected and willing to share the knowledge they have attained through years of experience. They didn't gain their insights and abilities overnight, and neither will you. You need to train with the best, take classes from top-level instructors, and work hard at gaining as much knowledge and skill as possible.

As you learn new skills, become a mentor yourself and share your skills with others. This will help you anchor your skills, improve your efficiency and build your reputation as a mentor. As time goes on, the knowledge you have to share will grow, as will your reputation as a mentor.

Mentoring means helping someone else achieve their version of success, helping them learn how to live in the world you share. This is the give and take of building a highly functioning team. Often, the role of mentor is held by the senior member of the team and not the ranking officer. Sometimes, the senior person will mentor the formal leader. In many of the positions I've held, someone I was charged with leading helped me develop as a leader. Their experience and knowledge base made it important for me to be open to their influence and instruction. Seeking input from these individuals not only added value to me, but to them as well. It also strengthened our relationship and built trust in one another.

I started mentoring others because mentoring plays a role in achieving proficiency in all other areas. Professional mentors help people achieve some predetermined goal. Spiritual mentors guide others to enlightenment, salvation, forgiveness, a better life, etc. In my experience, good mentors make the best teachers.

While knowing what to add is important, equally important is knowing what to take away. Everyone has weights and limitations. Recognizing the things that slow you down is key to reaching your goal.

What to Subtract

Do you have distractions and time wasters that drain away hours of your productivity every week? Maybe you need to cancel your Netflix subscription. Does noise and activity in your environment hinder your studies? Maybe you need to change the location of your computer from the kitchen desk to a corner of the basement. Do you have relationships that kill your drive, such as a friend who tells you you're living in a dream world because you want to be more? Maybe have a conversation to let them know you need less of that kind of talk in your relationship.

This takes you back to your spheres of control and influence.

You only have control over your own thoughts, behaviors and actions. You cannot control the thoughts, behaviors and actions of others. Instead of trying to control others, you can try to influence them. Sometimes that will work, but not always. This awareness will help you make adjustments that actually make a difference. Instead of trying to control a situation where you have no real ability to make a change, you can choose a different path to get where you want to go.

Epictetus was a Greek Stoic philosopher whose teachings were written down and compiled by his pupil Arrian in his *Discourses* and *Enchiridion*. Epictetus said that wisdom comes by determining what is within your control and what was not within your control. All external events are beyond your control, and you should accept them with indifference. However, you are responsible for your own actions.

He taught that the space between an event and acting upon it— the instant before you take action—is where you decide whether to be wise or unwise. Through self-discipline and self-leadership, you can make the right choice. That instant is within your sphere of control. That instant contains your opinions, impulses, desires and aversions. Not within your control is your body, possessions, glory and power. Any delusion on this point leads to the greatest errors, misfortunes, and troubles, and to the slavery of the soul.[40] You have no control over external things. The good that should to be your goal is only within yourself.[41] Focus your energy on the things you can change: your thoughts, your behaviors and your actions.

---

40 Heinrich Ritter, Alexander James William Morrison, *The History of Ancient Philosophy*, Vol 4, 204.
41 Ibid., 206.

"Focus your energy on the things you can change: your thoughts, your behaviors and your actions."

I addressed programming and limiting beliefs in Chapter 4 to show in detail that your own thinking is vitally important to your success. If you see yourself as unworthy, you will have a lot of resistance to advancing in your career and find it difficult to reach your goals. Mindset work is key to building forward momentum.

Right behind limiting beliefs comes self-sabotaging behavior. Look a little deeper into why you tend to say yes to a friend who invites you to party all weekend when you should be studying. Why do you order greasy, low-nutrient food that makes you feel sluggish instead of a nourishing meal that energizes your body? Why do you engage in risky social behaviors? Why do you want to coast instead of dig in and reach for your dreams? Yes, you need self-discipline, but if self-discipline seems impossible for you, your first step is to get help finding the underlying cause of your resistance and resolve that.

Distractions and time wasters happen to everyone. To minimize them, look at your physical environment. Have you set the stage for success? Is the TV always on in the background? Does your game controller stay next to your keyboard? If so, you have built-in distractions. Become aware of your surroundings and improve your environment.

This principle includes the people around you. For example, if your team at work is filled with gloom-and-doom thinkers who scoff at people who do their best, maybe you need to put in for a transfer. If your team hasn't made their stats for the past six quarters, maybe you should check out other options. Become aware of your work culture and the attitudes of your co-workers. Position yourself within a group that has upward momentum and you will find it much easier to rise.

At some point, everyone who follows their Grand Strategy will have to make a choice between their old life and their new goals. These are tough calls that will put your commitment and determination on the line. This includes relationships, both professional and personal.

As I've stated several times, relationships are vital to your success. Unhealthy relationships will hold you back, especially when those relationships involve over-responsibility. This can happen in two ways. First, where you feel too much responsibility for someone who is capable of taking care of themselves. You cannot control the thoughts, actions, and behaviors of anyone else, no matter how much you love them, worry about them or want the best for them. When you have no control, you need to let go of that feeling of responsibility. Holding on to it drains your energy and hinders your progress.

The second way over-responsibility happens is when someone feels too much responsibility for you and insists about what you should and shouldn't do. Allowing someone else to influence you in ways that hinder your upward progress is a test to your commitment.

To get clarity when you feel tugged in two directions, go back to your values and remember what is really important to you. The only right-or-wrong answer is whether you are staying true to your values or not. Your Grand Strategy might change. That's not necessarily a failure. It might be simply a course correction.

When relationships become too complicated, get counseling. Someone outside the situation can help you find your way. Counseling, coaching and mentoring are a repeating theme. You will need personal help from time to time. Plan on it. Accepting that kind of help is a sign of your dedication to your Grand Strategy and a sign that you are ready to face the reality of where you are now. When you are ready for the truth, the truth will set you free.

"Reality is truth, and what is true is so, regardless of whether we know it is, or are aware of that truth."
~Akṣapada Gautama[42]

"Every soul is deprived of the truth against its will."
~Plato[43]

While putting together your action steps, don't forget to include your contribution to others. Selfish Altruism creates wins on many levels. When you advance your own dreams while also helping others reach theirs, the benefits are vast and far-reaching.

Action Step 6: Create action steps.
Use the space below to list action steps in the areas of your career, your personal life, and your relationships. Once your lists are complete, in the next chapter you will prioritize your steps and add some dates. The accompanying workbook has more questions lined out in much greater detail, but the questions below will get you started.

    a.   What do you need to add? (education, environment, fitness, relationships, etc.)

       Career: _____

       _____

---

42 Jeaneane Fowler, 130.
43 Matthew Van Natta, *The Beginner's Guide to Stoicism: Tools for Emotional Resilience and Positivity*, 74.

Personal Life: _____

_____

Relationships: _____

_____

b. What do you need to subtract? (attitudes, habits, relationships, time-wasters, etc.)

Career: _____

_____

Personal Life: _____

_____

Relationships: _____

_____

c. What Selfish Altruism activities can you engage in
weekly?

_____

_____

_____

_____

_____

_____

CHAPTER 7:

Where Do You Begin?

B efore creating your action plan, make sure you are headed in the right direction. This means checking back through the Action Steps at the end of each chapter to see what might have changed since you began studying this material.

What obstacles did you list in Step 5? Sometimes you can overcome an obstacle or work around it, but sometimes you might need to take a completely different route.

One of my clients (I'll call her Sally, not her real name) was in law enforcement. She went into that field because her core values were justice, integrity and compassion. Helping people was part of who she was. She had studied psychology in college and was also an EMT. She had left her major because the field was so broad, she felt overwhelmed. She didn't know how to plug those skills into her life purpose. She entered the police academy for more hands-on involvement in saving lives and helping victims find justice.

At the beginning of our coaching program, she said she wanted to move up through the ranks as a police officer, so she could make a difference and help more people. Unfortunately, a big boulder stood in her way. The men she worked with made her life miserable. She was very capable, but every time she made an achievement, they would scorn her and make suggestive remarks about how she must be seducing the boss.

They continually gave her the worst jobs. She had sex crimes assigned to her because she was a woman. She had to watch every evidence video of child abuse that came into the department. She felt she had no voice to object because she would be labeled as weak if she refused.

Sally started dreading going to work. She developed PTSD from on-the-job trauma and also from the constant harassment of her male team members. Eventually, she had to admit she couldn't move that boulder. Every milestone she reached came with a social penalty in the form of harassment and innuendo. Add to that the challenges that come with police work and Sally was in a major struggle. She knew in that environment she couldn't keep her spirits up and maintain her drive over the long haul.

Her quality of life had gone down to the point where she had to take care of herself or be mowed under by the system. She took another look at her Grand Strategy and found dozens of other routes that would fulfill her purpose of helping people and take her to her End State. She added Quality of Life to her list of values and made some new choices.

Your purpose is not tied to one particular vocation. You can fulfill your purpose in dozens of ways. Obstacles are redirections, not the end of the road. Your occupation is simply one avenue of expression for your life purpose in the midst of many possible avenues.

"Your occupation is simply one avenue
of expression for your life purpose."

When you find a way to fulfill your purpose where the work itself is rewarding, you have found your sweet spot. You will get up every morning looking forward to the day. You will keep going despite sleepless nights, working in the heat or the cold and performing tasks that would overwhelm most people. You keep going because you love what you do. You'd do it even if you didn't get paid.

No more internal conversations about the company not doing enough for their employees, or the job taking a toll on your health. When you find a way to fulfill your purpose and make a comfortable living, you will feel a surge in energy. Everything will seem lighter. You will go above and beyond because you are acting from the core of who you are, not simply ticking off a list from your job description.

I talk to people all the time who started into a career and found out that the job didn't allow them to fulfill their purpose like they thought it would. For example, someone who wants to help veterans might get a job at the Veterans Administration with high hopes of helping veterans and their families. But, once inside, they find themselves buried in bureaucracy. Their daily tasks don't reflect their purpose. They might spend their days going to meetings and filing paperwork and seeing no real help for the people they came to serve. This leads to heaviness and a feeling of discontent. That's the time to take a look at possible aspects of the job that bring you the most fulfillment and see how you can focus more on that.

For Sally, her non-negotiable was helping people. She wanted to help those who can't help themselves and hold those accountable who harm the weak. She thought psychology would take her to her End State, but she didn't know how to proceed with that career. She thought becoming a police officer would take her to her End State, but she had obstacles in her way. However, her years on the police force gave her insight she didn't have before. She knew many police officers and EMTs who needed help with PTSD.

Sally came up with a viable solution. She joined her two fields together in a way that fulfilled her purpose and gave her a better quality of life. She decided to go back to school and become a licensed clinical social worker with a specific focus: first responders with PTSD.

Sally drew up a new action plan. What did she need to subtract from her life? Her idea that law enforcement was the best way for reaching her End State. She also subtracted the harassment and disrespect she endured on a daily basis. What did she need to add? More education and meeting the licensure requirements to become a social worker.

Not only was Sally happier in her new vocation, she also had more influence and helped far more people in real and tangible ways. Sally is on her way, learning and course correcting, narrowing down more and more to her sweet spot. Possibly a few years from now, she will discover a way to narrow down even more. Maybe she will remain a social worker until she retires. Either way, she will enjoy her life on the path to her End State.

Everyone goes through a maturing process where you work in a field and realize that some parts of it leave you energized at the end of the day. Other facets of the job aren't nearly as enjoyable.

If you are self-aware, over time you might make an adjustment, so you can put more focus on rewarding activities. This way, you eventually zero in on the tasks that bring you the most fulfillment.

This goes far beyond landing promotions with more pay and vacation time. This is creating your life based on your passion and purpose. You feel buoyancy and forward momentum because you are able to express the core of who you are, more and more as time goes by.

"This is creating your life based on
your passion and purpose."

Most of my life, my identity was wrapped up in my role as a firefighter and officer in the fire department. When I went through the DUI situation followed by an injury, I sank into depression. I couldn't imagine my life without the fire service. I spent years reestablishing myself in my career. That situation was more of a growth opportunity than an obstacle, although I didn't see it that way at the time. Do I regret my decision to hang in there and get back into the fire service? Not at all. I was on my path, and I loved it.

Years later, I ran into a different challenge in the fire service. By that time, I had enough personal development and self-awareness to take an honest look at my core values, my purpose and my goals. I realized that what I loved the most about my leadership position within the fire service was coaching. So, I narrowed my focus to coaching. Now, I have a coaching practice and a podcast that reaches far beyond the fire service. I'm helping more people than ever—while still making progress toward my End State. That's what the Grand Strategy is all about.

Personal development sometimes prompts people to change paths, even without outside events. Maybe their first goal was in response to some past trauma, such as a victim of domestic violence working in a shelter for battered women. When that person is able to work through their past trauma, they might realize that they are stuck in a reactive space with a need to continually fight the negative. Personal development and self-awareness would allow them to find their life purpose and the courage to follow their true passion. They have the freedom to reach for their full potential.

---

*"Personal development and self-awareness
allow them to find their life purpose and the
courage to follow their true passion."*

Someone close to me (I'll call him Alex, not his real name) started out by joining a high school vocational program in the field of hospitality engineering. He was good with his hands, so he figured he would get good grades. After school, a large hotel chain hired him. Alex had no real passion for his career, but he was excellent at it. He rose through the ranks and eventually changed companies to become the property manager of high-profile vacation condos with a wealthy clientele.

Alex was making a good income. He had security and respect from his superiors and the gratitude of people in the condo complex. However, after a few years, he felt dissatisfied. Something inside him said his life could be more fulfilling. When he expressed this to me, I loaned him some personal development books. Although he was not a client, we had some meaningful discussions about passion and purpose.

In his new awareness, Alex thought about the frustration of the condo owners when they commissioned work at a high rate and received cheap, shoddy products in return. Because of his role in the complex, he knew a lot of these people.

Alex decided to start his own company. He would own a property management company as well as take commissions for custom woodworking. Giving up his job security seemed like a leap of faith, but Alex knew he was on the right track, and he plunged right in. Today, he is living life on his own terms, hiring good people to take care of property management and enjoying his woodworking shop. He takes pride in his craftsmanship and goes beyond his clients' expectations because he loves what he does. Word has gotten out among the wealthy community in Florida, and he stays busy.

Although his parents did not support his dream, he had encouragement and advice from others. He found a support network. Alex is living in his sweet spot where he does what he loves, the work itself is rewarding, and he makes a good living at the same time.

Some people realize their original goal wasn't their own, but the dream a parent or teacher had for them. Personal development would bring this to light, resulting in a change in their Grand Strategy. You can't live someone else's dream and feel fulfilled. With clarity comes the opportunity to make your own choices and live your life as an empowered individual.

This often happens when the family owns a business. The younger generation feels immense pressure to take over the business when their elders become too old to continue, especially if the business has given the family a high standard of living for thirty years, fifty years or even more. The family can't imagine letting it go or selling it.

This happened to a friend of mine in south Florida who came from a very successful family. Luis (not his real name) had a conversation with his uncle, who invited him into the family business. His uncle paid for his education and completely set him up with an outfitted office, established clientele, and seven figures in startup money. Luis enjoyed the work at first, but after a while he realized that the family business wasn't his passion. He wanted to be a pilot.

During his free time, he took flying lessons and put in his flight hours. He found people to take over more and more of his responsibilities at the office and put more time into flying. Currently, he has a business manager taking care of the office while he flies for a private jet company taking multi-millionaires around the world. Luis is living his dream where he's following his passion, the work itself is rewarding, and he's making a nice living doing it. In Luis's case, he was able to keep the family business going and follow his dream at the same time.

Life is all about options and possibilities. Many times, the biggest obstacle you will come against is within your own thinking. Luis had the vision to delegate what he didn't want to do. He subtracted some office activities from his own calendar and gave those to someone else. Then, he had time to add what he loved: flying. With his entrepreneurial mindset, he also figured out how to make money at the same time.

What about you? Do you have a boulder in your path? Are you allowing an obstacle to prevent you from moving forward? In my coaching practice, if someone is stalled, most of the time they already know the solution, but they don't want to do what it takes to move forward.

> *"If someone is stalled, most of the time they already know the solution, but they don't want to do what it takes to move forward."*

One of the most difficult obstacles to overcome is a relationship that is holding you back. Who has you within their circle of influence? This could be a spouse or significant other, friends, grown children—the list goes on. Do those people use their influence to support you, or do they try to control you and hold you to their expectations?

If someone important to you does not agree with your chosen path, take a good look at your priorities. Can you maintain your core values and head toward your goal while also keeping that person happy? Can you find a path you would enjoy on the way to your End State while also easing your relationship? Take the time to fully explore your options. You might find an opportunity you love that makes your loved one happy as well. Ask yourself if you can modify your End State and still feel happy and fulfilled.

The key is to remain true to your core values and your purpose. If you have to compromise your non-negotiables to make someone else happy, that relationship needs a closer look. Healthy relationships create a win-win for both people.

These are questions only you can answer, and you can only answer them if you are clear on what you stand for and what you want your life to mean. You can only answer them if you answer the hard questions with complete honesty.

Going back to your list of values and goals:

- Which are non-negotiable?
- Which can be modified?
- Which can be eliminated?

Your non-negotiables are not up for discussion. Whether you figure it out now or ten years from now, you have to live your life, not somebody else's version of it. You can drag someone along. You can hang back with them and give up on what you know would be fulfilling for you, or you can communicate effectively with them and share why it's so important for you to follow your path. If they are who you need them to be at that moment in time, not only will they walk with you, but they will put you up on their shoulders.

The other person in your relationship also needs to live their own life, and not your version of it. If you don't agree with what they are doing, they might not see some pitfalls that you see. Possibly you can communicate your experience to them and support them in that way. However, if they feel strongly that they are on the path to fulfilling their life purpose, then you should support them in following their dreams as well.

Healthy relationships are not about control. They are about support and understanding, regardless of whether everyone shares the same passion or not.

"Healthy relationships are not about control."

In a stressful situation where someone close to you does not support you in something as important as your Grand Strategy and reaching your End State, their doubts will amplify your doubts and cause you to stall. Without a change, the disconnection between the two of you will become more and more apparent over time.

Whether your significant other, your parent, your adult children or your friends—if someone continually bashes your dreams, that relationship is in jeopardy. Either one or both of you will develop resentment. Even if you stay in the relationship, the good parts will eventually disappear. People in this situation often end up going their separate ways after years of struggle.

Yes, this is hard to face. It is painful. Unfortunately, it will be more painful the longer you wait, so don't wait another ten years to take action. Work on repairing that relationship, whether through counseling or some other means. If nothing helps to bring about the changes you need, in order to continue following your Grand Strategy, you will need to explore other options.

First and foremost, make a commitment to live your life full out by following your purpose wholeheartedly, without reservation. Seek out others who have been where you are. Find a mentor, a coach or a friend who has the kind of experience you don't have. Read about people who have tried what you are doing and failed. Learn from their mistakes. Go back to the philosophers and imbibe their wisdom. Learn from others so you can easily achieve what others have labored hard for.

"Employ your time in improving yourself by other men's writings, so that you shall gain easily what others have labored hard for."
~Socrates

Relationships can be positive and supportive. They can also be negative and draining. When you make a commitment to your Grand Strategy, you will inevitably come to the point where you need to enroll others into your plan. Regardless of what others might say or do, the most important question is: How firm is your resolve to do what it takes to reach your End State?

---

*"How firm is your resolve to do what it takes
to reach your End State?"*

If you don't have support now, create it. Develop a network that will cheer you on and celebrate every milestone with you. Subtract what you don't want, and add what you do want. Make a space where you can thrive.

Action Step 7: Revisit your goals.
Now that you have been through these steps, check in to see if you need to make modifications based on what you have learned.

1. Which goals are non-negotiable? _____

   _____

2. Which can be modified? _____

   _____

3. Which can be eliminated? _____

   _____

4. Which goals should be completed first? _____

   _____

5. Which of your goals need the enrollment of others? Do you have their enrollment or not? _____

   _____

   _____

6. What steps can you take to strengthen your support network? _____

You can find multiple resources to help you at: www.HollenbachLeadership.com/coaching-mentoring.

CHAPTER 8:

What's Your Timeline?

With your top priorities in mind, it's time to make a practical plan to reach your End State. Like a map for a road trip, this involves three foundational questions:

1. Where are you now?
2. Where do you want to end up?
3. What route will you take to get there?

For someone in the fire department I would ask, "What rank are you now and what rank do you want to retire at?" When they give me their answer—say, Captain—I reply, "Let's go two ranks higher than that." I recommend pushing out the limits a little bit. This person might have the potential to go further than they think.

Maybe they will do more with their extra time near the end. Also, if a delay happens at some point, they will still be okay.

In my old department the rank above Captain is Battalion Chief and above that is Assistant Chief. Looking at Assistant Chief, we would go back to where the client is now. We will then look at education requirements, experience requirements, technical training and any other requirements. With the major milestones in place, we again go back to the beginning and line out the steps for each milestone. A spreadsheet works well for this because you can add rows when you need them.

If you need a Master's Degree, you must complete your Bachelor's Degree at least two years earlier. I would begin by asking if you have any college credits already completed, and what local or online courses are available, so you can make definite plans.

If you work full time and you have a family, you might need more time to complete your courses. Or you can save up vacation weeks, enter an accelerated program and knock out the degree with focused work in short bursts. By taking work styles and time constraints into account, you can come up with a plan and a timeline.

Once that is in place, you can get down to the details of how many hours per week do you have available to study? How many hours can you free up? For example, if you currently spend four hours a week on lawncare, you might hire someone to do your yard instead. The same is true for dog walking and having your groceries delivered instead of driving to the store.

If you spend two hours a night playing video games, you can use that time to study or enroll in a class. However, schedule changes can get tricky. If you play video games with family members, eliminating your play time is not necessarily a given. Family time is important and should remain on your schedule, although possibly shortened. Down time is also important. If you need to spend three hours playing a video game on Friday nights to unwind after a long week, eliminating that segment of time could put you into burnout.

Your life is multidimensional. You need time for yourself and time for your family. You need social interaction and play time. You need to make a contribution to others and your community. You also need quiet for meditation and time to exercise. All of these are important. You are entering an epic journey that will last for years, even decades, so pace yourself. Along with your education and learning requirements, here are other areas that you will want to include as you build your plan.

"You are entering an epic journey that will last for years, so pace yourself."

Finances

Your finances are an important aspect in your path to your End State. If your finances are like a boat taking on water and you have to keep bailing to stay afloat, whether you reach your goal of Captain or not, your retirement years will not be what you imagine. Finances can put stress on your relationships as well. If you are maxed out in debt and your credit score is low, you might need to plan for your financial recovery before beginning any additional schooling. You might need to seek financial counseling while you look for financial aid to cover your education costs. Money is a mindset. Many times, you can adjust your situation simply by paying attention.

Relationships

Relationships are an important part of your daily, weekly and monthly routine. Starting with where your relationships are right now, what actions can you take to improve them? If your time for meaningful conversations with your children happens in the car while you drive them home from sports practice, by all means don't free up that time by asking someone else to drive them or by putting in earbuds to listen to a study recording while you are with them. Although you might be busy, by staying aware you can make the most of your time with your family and keep your relationships solid.

Are you spending quality time with your spouse or significant other? Are you communicating effectively, both listening and speaking? If you allow your relationship to end up on the rocks or if you lose connection with your children because your focus stays on other things, what real benefit will promotions at work bring to you? Again, your core values and priorities should always come into the equation when making plans and instituting changes.

Your support network is important. If your primary relationships are not on board with your goals, your daily challenges become exponentially tougher. Not many people have the energy or the drive to fight someone else while they also practice self-leadership to keep going when they feel tired or discouraged. You also need time and focus for your own self-care, and a troubled relationship will take a heavy toll on your ability to do that.

At the same time, if your significant other starts out as supportive, then communicates that your plan is causing them a lot of stress, the first step is to listen and try to work with them to make adjustments that will ease their stress. Every time you have a change, such as finishing one goal and beginning the next one, you will have course corrections to make. When people around you want you to succeed, these conversations can deepen and strengthen your relationships—as long as they understand that you are listening and you have their best interest at heart.

Personality styles and communication styles come into play as you work through these adjustments. In my coaching, I sometimes use a tool such as the DISC Assessment to help my client understand how to express what they want to say in a way that their family members can relate to. If you want someone to understand you, you must speak their language.

"If you want someone to understand you, you must speak their language."

You must also set aside adequate time to allow the other person to formulate their thoughts and express their needs back to you. When you have your Grand Strategy in place with your goals and timelines, you might feel rushed at times. However, rushing all the time is not helpful. When you are with someone important to you, be with them without a sense of urgency to get to the next thing. Give them the gift of your full, unhurried attention.

In the middle of reaching your deadlines, don't forget to value time spent on your relationships and maintaining your finances. The same is true for your own mental, physical and spiritual health.

Your Health and Wellness

When you create your daily and weekly plans, make a space for your mental, physical and spiritual wellbeing. A daily Tactical Pause is important. Exercise is important. Good food is important. You don't have to do a lot every day, but you should do at least a little, whether in the morning, on your lunch hour or in the evening. Here's where you need dedication and discipline to make this an integral part of your normal routine. I go into this in more detail in Chapter 9.

Contribution is also important to your wellbeing. Whenever you can, complete your tasks while practicing Selfish Altruism, helping others as you also reach your own goals. Mentoring others at work is an example of a good way to make a contribution while also maximizing the use of your time. The intrinsic rewards that come with helping others will help you stay motivated over the long term.

When you are planning the various aspects of your self-care, choose things you enjoy. Make this part of your life a series of rewards you look forward to. Also, plan for down times. Set aside time for vacations, play days and rest days. Your Grand Strategy might take you two or more decades to complete. If your months and years contain nothing but urgency and stress, you will be less likely to reach your End State, and even if you do, your quality of life won't be what you envisioned when you started out.

This is a balancing act. When your financial, physical and spiritual health are strong, your relationships will strengthen as well. With every adjustment, you will encounter benefits and drawbacks. By weighing those out, you can come up with the best scenarios possible for you at any given time. Coaching is important for navigating this process. Someone outside your sphere will see things you don't see and have insights you won't realize. At the very least, check out the workbook companion to this publication with more help to get you on track and keep you going.

Plan for adjustments and modifications. What you have in mind as you set up your daily and weekly schedule will often not happen in the way you imagined. For example, you might plan to study for an hour on Tuesday nights. However, your daughter struggles with math and she has a weekly math quiz on Wednesdays, so you need to spend that hour on Tuesday evenings with her instead. Until you put your plan into play, you won't realize the hidden factors that shape your day. Also, people often underestimate how much time tasks actually take. Course corrections are a normal part of the process, not a place to feel frustration or anxiety.

"Course corrections are a normal part of the process, not a place to feel frustration or anxiety."

Schedule regular check-ins, especially when you first begin to implement your strategy. After you settle into a routine, revisit your schedule every few weeks to remove any drift that might have happened and to look for stress points for both you and your family members. Then, simply make your adjustments and try again.

Stay alert for signs of internal stress such as tightness in your chest or gut. Watch out for sinking feelings and negative thoughts. As long as you are present to how you feel, these signposts will notify you that you need to check in. You need to find out more about what is going on, so you can take care of it before you have bigger problems to deal with.

For example, maybe your spouse is distant and short with you in the evening and again in the morning. On the drive to work you feel nagging tightness in your chest, and you have trouble focusing on your driving-time audiobook. Instead of blaming yourself for lack of discipline, notice where that tension is coming from.

Keeping short accounts will prevent relationship problems from escalating. You can give your spouse a call or seek them out when you get home to discover what's on their mind and how you can support them. Their situation might have nothing to do with you, but keeping the relationship open and supportive helps everyone involved. Take the time to build relationship equity, so you, as a couple, can withstand stressors that will happen down the road.

Compiling your Grand Strategy into written form is a big undertaking with many levels and many facets. I like using a spreadsheet because this is a fluid, organic process that continually shifts and changes as you shift and change. A spreadsheet will allow you to add or remove sections as you need to.

Following your Grand Strategy is so much more than reaching a list of goals. You are growing into who you want to be, molding yourself into the person who not only attains the higher ranks but who also fulfills roles that require greater and greater responsibility. You are developing maturity to fit into the End State you have chosen for yourself. Along with dedication and commitment, you will also need to be patient with your growing pains and allow yourself to stumble sometimes as you gain experience and learn from the school of hard knocks.

"Be patient with your growing pains and allow yourself to stumble sometimes as you gain experience."

Emotional resistance will come up as you go through this planning process. For example, you might experience a rush of dread when you sit down to examine your finances. You might feel overwhelmed when you see how much you need to accomplish in the next year. When those responses happen, first of all realize that those feelings come from being too dialed in on one detail. You need to take a step back to see the bigger picture and bring yourself back to calm focus. With awareness, you can resolve those feelings and keep making progress. Here are some tools to help you:

Box Breathing during a Tactical Pause

Box Breathing is a highly effective tool used by Navy SEALS to move themselves from overwhelm into a state of deep calm with increased focus. Whenever your heart rate goes up, and you feel scattered, take a few seconds to quiet yourself. If you allow overwhelm to overtake you, your only recourse will be to step away altogether and come back at a later time.

Here's how to do it:

1. Close your eyes. Breathe in through your nose while counting slowly to 4.
2. Hold your breath while counting slowly to 4.
3. Slowly exhale for a count of 4.
4. Hold your breath again for a count of 4.
5. Repeat at least three more times for a total of 4 repetitions.

I call this a Tactical Pause because it's a simple way to bring yourself into the present and get back on track. Afterward, journal about what happened, how you felt about what happened and how you resolved it. If that sounds to touchy-feely, just make a journal entry regarding what led to your desire to take a Tactical Pause, the mental and physiological effects upon doing so, and how you approached the same task afterward.

Emotional Freedom Technique (Tapping)

Tapping has been around for more than twenty-five years. Through a series of gentle taps with the fingertips on the face, head and chest, you can quickly release anxiety and dissolve resistance. Many videos on YouTube demonstrate how to do this simple technique. Tapping is good for dissolving old negative energy and adjusting your mindset. When you feel stuck in a pattern of behavior that doesn't work for you any more, tapping is the place to begin.

Forgiveness work

Forgiveness is a process of releasing yourself from anger and other negative emotions that stay with you after a difficult event is over. Unresolved negative emotions leave you with triggers that will hinder your progress. If you have difficulty letting those feelings go, seek out a coach or counselor. Sometimes tapping can also help.

If you are like me and you don't like the thought of forgiving certain people. Understand, that this practice isn't meant to absolve someone of their wrongdoing. It is meant to release the negativity that comes with thinking about that person or what they did. It is for you, not them.

Journaling

A daily journaling practice has tremendous benefits. I go into more detail on journaling in the next chapter.

Moving your body

Positive endorphins flow into your body as you move and exercise. Give yourself the gift of feeling better by simply moving, whether you practice yoga, go through a workout routine or dance.

Walk outdoors and then come back to the issue

Taking a break in the fresh air will do wonders for giving you a new perspective. Step away for a few minutes, and you will come back with renewed energy.

Working your Grand Strategy requires commitment and self-management. Use these tools when you feel pressed or stressed. They are a powerful way to help you see and achieve success.

Let's face it. We're all human. Sometimes you won't feel like doing what you need to do. Sometimes you will doubt yourself and wonder if you'll ever get where you want to go. Sometimes, you might even consider quitting. That's why regular check-ins are important. You will need to remind yourself that you didn't choose this path because it is easy. You chose it because it is right for you and your family. Your community and the world will be a better place because of your dedication and leadership.

Growth of any kind causes discomfort. A few months back, I went to a personal development retreat where I learned how to forge a railroad spike into a knife. The first step was to heat the steel until it glowed red hot in the forge. I pounded the hot spike with a four-pound hammer until it cooled off. Then the spike went back into the heat until it glowed red hot again. I hammered it again, and again, and again until it was the size and shape I wanted.

Imagine, if that railroad spike could talk, what would it have said during that long process? Possibly it would have breathed a sigh of relief when it finally reached the size and shape of a knife, but that was just the start. It had to go yet another round in the forge to temper the steel and harden it. After that, the new knife had to be polished and sharpened.

"Growth of any kind causes discomfort."

Maturity takes time. Wisdom comes from making mistakes, taking the heat and refining your understanding of how the world works. You learn, you improve, and you stay in the game.

With your Grand Strategy in place, you are more prepared than most, knowing you chose this path. You have a firm resolve to define yourself based on your values and your purpose, rather than let someone else define you. You want your name to mean something to those who come after you. No matter how hot the forge gets, you will go the distance.

Action Step 8: Set up your Grand Strategy spreadsheet

Create a spreadsheet for your Grand Strategy. You can also create a table in your word processing program or start with lined paper and a pencil. Here is an example of big-picture planning for someone in law enforcement.

Donut Eater Career Path Goals with Actionable Strategy								
Daily:	Journal: https://dailystoic.com/stoic-art-of-journaling/	Meditate: https://livepurposefullynow.com/gratitude-meditations/	Academic or Skill Based Study	Read Something to Improve Skills and/or Knowledge	Exercise for 30 minutes/minimum			
Weekly:	Study/Review LEO Best Practices and Changes to Law	Study EMS Based Protocols	Study Leadership Materials/Literature	Seek Out Opportunities to Add Value to Someone	Coaching Call			
Monthly:	Confirm your weekly goals are being achieved	School/Training	Call Mentor					
Quarterly:	Review and edit Longterm Goals	Meet with Mentor to Review Goals and Professional Development Strategy	Read Previous Quarter's Journal Entries					
Annually:								
3 Years:	Investigator							
4Years:	Instructor	Start BA/BS degree						
8 Years:	Lieutenant	Complete BA/BS degree	Start MA/MS degree					
15 Years:	Chief Of Police							

1. As you can see, at three years, he wanted to achieve the rank of Investigator. On your own spreadsheet, list your major milestones with a timeline for each.
2. Next to those major milestones, list the requirements you still need to do.
3. Include your financial goals, such as paying off debt by a certain date.
4. Let the document rest for a day or two, then come back and look at it again to catch anything you might have missed.
5. Set your start date and pull the trigger.

CHAPTER 9:

What's Your Daily Routine?

In any profession, most seasoned veterans are sticklers about certain details. Rookies often get frustrated over those same details. This tension has been around for so long that it has become something of a cliché. The drill sergeant in movies is always shouting at the raw recruits because of something they did sloppily or something they forgot. Those recruits don't realize that their success depends on small actions and repetitive processes. That's right. The boring stuff. However, when you have enough experience to know the difference, those things are no longer quite so boring.

Prior to beginning my career in the fire service, I was in the Navy. My time in the Navy gave me a clear understanding of why attention to detail is so important. Early on, we had this drilled into our brain with "ridiculous" drills and inspections. We would be inspected for how we were groomed and how we wore our uniforms. Our lockers were inspected and our clothes were to be folded in a very specific way. If our underwear wasn't folded perfectly, everything in our locker would be thrown on the deck and corrective physical training would begin.

In dangerous environments, attention to detail can mean the difference between life and death. In a structure fire, how you have maintained your gear, how you have donned it, and how you conduct a search in zero visibility can determine whether you find the resident that didn't make it out, whether you get burned, or whether your breathing apparatus functions as it is supposed to and keeps you alive. Most of these details come down to forming good habits.

Once you have begun a bad habit, research shows it takes 3,000-5,000 repetitions to overcome it. However, if you practice the proper technique or behavior from the start, you will only need 300-500 repetitions to form a fresh habit. "A study in the *European Journal of Social Psychology* analyzed the habits of 96 people over 12 weeks. On average, it is said that a habit takes around 2 months to become an automatic behavior—66 days to be exact. And for some it can take up to eight months."[44]

Some habits involve developing muscle memory. Some rewire neuron circuits in the brain. Give yourself time to develop the changes you want without judgment. Put in your reps and allow the change to develop.

As I am writing this, one of my personal goals is to become more mindful than I was the day before, to stay present and aware. Every time I find myself zoning out or having a knee-jerk reaction, I bring myself back to being present. Once I have achieved my

---

44 Seana, "Habit formation: Is 21 days all it takes?"

mindfulness habit, I will continue to reinforce it until it becomes an instilled behavior, an automatic response. When I no longer have to think about it and bring myself back to present, the mindfulness habit will be part of me.

On your journey to your End State, you will need to develop new habits. I have listed several below. None of these habits are time consuming or difficult, yet they are often ignored. Make a commitment that you will start your reps first thing tomorrow morning and keep on going until these are as natural to you as finding the off button on your alarm.

When You Wake Up

Fatigue, family stress and time pressure will hit you at a time of day when most people have little willpower—first thing in the morning. You'll have to go through the discomfort of changing your first-morning behaviors as you establish your new routine. With that in mind, do whatever you can to ease your way through this important transition.

Before you go to bed at night, prepare for the morning. Maybe you'll need to get up before your family does. Maybe you can take care of some of your current morning tasks before bed, such as making the kids' school lunches or having clothes ready to grab and pull on. Maybe the only change is a matter of renewing your intention to follow through with your new habits.

Whatever you need to do, make your plan and stick to it. The first twenty minutes of your day can mean the difference between reaching your End State or not. Truly, I can't emphasize this enough. Olympians start their day before dawn for a reason. They are self-motivated self-leaders. So, are you.

Some people feel better exercising when they first wake up because exercise helps them become alert and get their day started.

Some prefer Quiet Time for the first few minutes. Some want coffee and then Quiet Time. The order isn't as important as creating a morning flow that is workable for you. If exercise first thing in the morning gives you a headache, then go for Quiet Time first and exercise afterward. Support yourself to achieve success.

Exercise

At some points in my career, I could only do 5-10 minutes of exercise in the morning. I would set an interval timer on my phone, then get in as many pushups, sit ups and air squats as I could. When the timer went off, I hit the shower.

Back then, my fitness goal narrowed down to simply getting my blood moving and working up a sweat. On the other hand, if you work remotely possibly a rowing machine in the corner of your home office would be a good way to blow off steam between meetings. Find something you enjoy that works for you. Some of my clients prefer to run in place or do burpees for five minutes. Others do yoga poses. If you enjoy an activity that gets your body moving, do that. The only way you can get this wrong is by failing to do it at all.

I've had people ask me if walking their dog counts as exercise. My answer: if you're moving fast enough to get your blood pumping and a sweat going. To me, walking the dog is more meditative, but meditation is important, too.

Meditation and The Tactical Pause

During those busy years early on, I thought I was too busy for meditation. After a while, I became mentally and spiritually fatigued. I realized something had to change if I were to keep on going. Five minutes of meditation is far better than no meditation at all. Keep a meditation app or audio file on your phone, so at least once a day, preferably in the morning, you can kick back and strengthen who you are on the inside.

The purpose of meditation is to quiet the mind and create mental clarity. We're talking about spending just 5-10 minutes on this part of your morning routine. However, be aware that when you are pushing a time limit, you immediately face a dilemma. A ticking clock will sabotage your results. When you first get started, you will need to learn how to be fully present for only 5-10 minutes. Feeling pressured when you are in a rush will raise your blood pressure and increases your heart rate. If setting a timer for your meditation causes anxiety that's the opposite of what meditation is supposed to do for you.

Being fully present means the clock disappears from your thinking. You trust your alarm to get your attention when your meditation time is finished. Until then, let yourself float into the gentle music, the guided meditation or even the sound of your own voice repeating a mantra or affirmation. Let yourself float with no sense of urgency. This is your time to take care of yourself. Let it be your private oasis, your refuge. If all you get to do at first is breathe deeply, then give yourself credit for progress and keep on practicing.

Once you have become accustomed to deep breathing and relaxation, bring up your intention for the day. Let your intention come into your awareness and then let it drift away as you bring your mind back to quiet. In this space of calm, answers might come up or creative ideas might spark in your mind. Keep your journal handy to note these down, so you can let them go and keep coming back to peace. The same way you exercise to get your body energized, you need this quiet time to slow your breathing and heart rate to support and nourish your spiritual self, the person you are inside. This is where you get your focus and grounding for the day.

Any time I feel a little overwhelmed with a situation I utilize a practice that was taught to me in the fire service called the Tactical Pause. Whenever an incident commander in the fire service has a complex situation, the details can become overwhelming, especially within the first ten minutes on the scene. Many people are assembling. Crews are setting up. Law enforcement is on the scene as well as paramedics for medical intervention. The buildup of resources at the beginning of a large incident has a lot of moving parts and dozens of decisions made by many different people with different agendas.

In this situation, whenever an incident commander feels an increase in heartrate and a sense of mental overwhelm, the first thing to do is literally take a step back from the command post and draw in three deep breaths (a Tactical Pause). If three deep breaths aren't enough, take three more and evaluate the current conditions, actions underway to make the current conditions better, and what needs should be addressed. Called a C.A.N. report (Conditions, Actions, Needs), this is a quick way to gather your thoughts and assess the situation in order to make it better. I recommend the Tactical Pause and C.A.N. report to my coaching clients whenever they face a complex situation or whenever they feel a sense of overwhelm.

The beauty of the C.A.N. report is that it also works when thinking through your day. You can go through the steps mentally or make 3 columns in your journal and write them down.

- C-Conditions: What are the current conditions I should address?
- A-Actions: What actions are underway to change these conditions?

- N-Needs: What additional resources do I need to improve conditions further?

If you come across something that overwhelms you, start over. Close your eyes. Take three deep breaths, then go through these three categories again. From a calm, focused place the answers will come to you more quickly and easily. You can use the Tactical Pause any time you feel overwhelmed or confused about your next step. Note: if time is available, box breathing brings about clarity much quicker.

Daily Reading

Each morning, read something uplifting that will give you a thought for the day. This could be a spiritual text such as the Bible or an inspirational book of quotes. It could be a biographical book such as Autobiography of a Yogi by Yogananda or a philosophical work such as Meditations by Marcus Aurelius. When you read a thought that moves you, write that thought in your journal. Spend a moment contemplating what that thought means to you and how to apply it.

Journaling

Journaling is integral to your daily routine, both morning and evening. Not only is it a record of your challenges, your ideas and your observations, it also provides a brain dump that helps get repetitive thoughts off your mind, so you can be fully present. Your journal helps you keep certain items in the front of your mind. It reminds you of your mindset and your goals for the day.

This practice started hundreds of years ago. The Stoic philosopher Seneca recommended beginning the day by writing down what you hope to achieve that day along with some pieces of wisdom you would like to keep in your thoughts. When a routine has been around that long, and it is still followed by successful people today, there has to be a good reason for it. Journaling works.

A strong morning routine including journaling is a universal practice followed by some of history's greatest thinkers and philosophers from antiquity until today. It has benefits for every walk of life and area of expertise. History is full of examples of those who failed to recognize its importance. Make a firm commitment that you will follow through until this becomes a habit, then such a part of your normal day that you do it as naturally as putting on your socks.

I recommend using paper and pen for journaling. The brain engages differently when you write something out longhand. Typing on a keyboard doesn't have the same benefits.

To recap, your morning journaling should include the following:

1. Any ideas that surface during your Quiet Time
2. Thoughts from your Tactical Pause
3. An inspirational statement from your reading
4. A list of what you are grateful for (at least 3 things)

Finish your morning journaling with gratitude. Let that warm feeling fill your chest and remember how blessed you are. Using this method, you are journaling while you are also meditating and while you are reading, so most days this important segment will take only a few minutes.

If you stick to a plan and use a timer, you can start your day feeling energized, calm and focused by adding as few as twenty minutes to your current morning routine.

During the Day

More extensive journaling goes back to the time of the Stoics. Most of the world's great leaders journaled regularly. The Roman emperor Marcus Aurelius journaled throughout his reign. Although his journals were private during his lifetime, they were published under the title *Meditations* and can still be read today.

In a free-flow style, use journaling to explore your options when you are making decisions. Your answers aren't always linear. Sometimes writing will bring solutions to the surface that you won't be able to access another way. You are entering into your Grand Strategy. That means going beyond your current train of thought and expanding your mind to new ways of thinking and being. Journaling will help you.

"Sometimes writing will bring solutions to the surface that you won't be able to access another way."

Sun Tzu was a Chinese general, military strategist, writer and philosopher who lived around 500 B.C. Sun Tzu is traditionally credited as the author of the strategy classic, *The Art of War*, which influenced both Western and East Asian philosophy and military thinking. From the title, you might assume the book is about fighting, but the focus is more on alternatives to battle, such as stratagem, delay, the use of spies and alternatives to war by making and keeping alliances, the use of deceit and a willingness to submit, at least temporarily, to more powerful foes.[45]

---

45   John Carman & Anthony Harding (ed.), *Ancient Warfare*, 41.

Sun Tzu is revered around the world. During the twentieth century, *The Art of War* grew in popularity and saw practical use in Western society. It continues to influence many competitive endeavors to this day, including culture, politics, business and sports, as well as modern warfare[46]. Most schools that teach any form of strategy, including Yale's Grand Strategy curriculum, have *The Art of War* as required reading.

Sun Tzu is a stellar example of someone who expanded his thinking and wrote down his thoughts. He allowed solutions to appear in ways that were unusual and unexpected, and he changed the world.

Another method of journaling is asking a series of questions, known as the Socratic Method. The Greek philosopher Socrates was one of the founders of Western philosophy and the first moral philosopher of the Western ethical tradition of thought.[47] The Socratic Method broke a problem down into a series of questions. The questions would distill the answers closer and closer until they reached a primary truth. Using questions, you can explore your thoughts and get to the source of any problem. You can also break down complex issues and come to a reasonable solution.

Before Bed

The second vital part of your daily routine is the last few minutes before you retire. This is a time to wind down and look back over your day. The Stoic philosopher, Seneca, recommended journaling before bed to write down your successes and where you would like to do better in the future. You might also include lessons you might have learned that day or thoughts to help you when

---

46   "Sun Tzu," Wikipedia.com.
47   Gregory Vlastos, *Socrates, Ironist and Moral Philosopher*, 43.

faced with similar situations. The entry before bed is a way to balance the ledger for that day and put to rest any lingering thoughts, so you can have better sleep.

End the night's journal entry with gratitude. Praise yourself for what you did well and remind yourself of the good things in your life.

To recap, your nighttime journaling should include:

1. Your successes for that day
2. Where you would like to do better in the future
3. Lessons you learned that day
4. Thoughts to help you when faced with a similar situation
5. What you are grateful for (at least 3)

Regular Check-ins

Along with your daily check-in through journaling, schedule time to look back over your month, the last quarter and the year. On check-in days, you will page back through your journal and also look at your Grand Strategy spreadsheet[48] to ask these questions:

- Where are you in achieving your goals? Are you ahead of schedule? Behind schedule?
- Are you still on the path you laid out, or have you drifted?
- Do you still want to be on the original path, or do you want to make some changes?
- Do you feel fulfilled in your current roles?
- How are your relationships? Your finances? Your health? What could make them better?
- What are your next short-term goals?

---

48 Find more resources at Hollenbach Leadership 360.

You cannot drive a car without adjusting the steering wheel every few seconds. If you get distracted, you could end up in the ditch or, worse, in oncoming traffic. The same is true of your Grand Strategy. Regular check-ins are the same as adjusting the steering wheel. Whenever you check in, take the time to revisit your list of values and your purpose. Revisit your End State and what you want to have in place by then. Take a look at how you are going to get from where you are to where you want to end up.

Your life is multifaceted. Becoming hyper-focused is a pitfall of being on a path with strong goals. During your check-ins, look at all areas of your life and notice what you might have neglected or put off until later. Make sure you are employing Selfish Altruism as much as possible and that you are taking care of yourself. While you're at it, don't forget to have some fun and enjoy the ride.

Action Step 9: Create your daily routine.

What is your current morning routine?

- _____
- _____
- _____
- _____

How can you adjust your morning routine to include the four elements of exercise, meditation, reading and journaling?

_____
_____
_____
_____
_____
_____

CHAPTER 10:

When Everything Falls Apart

P eter Andrews loved his horses. He owned Tarwyn Park, a large ranch east of Canberra, the capitol of Australia in New South Wales, where his primary purpose was raising the fastest race-horses in Australia. Unfortunately, Australia had been in drought conditions for years, and his fields had dried up. Peter realized the landscape needed to return to its original condition—the way it was hundreds of years ago—if his horses were to perform to their maximum. He decided to make changes on his own property and turn back the clock to when streams and ponds dotted the fields, to when thick grass covered the countryside and wildlife was everywhere.

He studied the flow of water across his property. He learned about soil quality and what it takes to slow down the water long enough to restore the ground cover. He spent month after month digging ditches and creating swales to allow water to sink deeply into the soil. He dealt with angry neighbors and threatening government officials who only saw that he was doing things differently and didn't appreciate that his acreage was becoming greener and more inviting.

Over the next thirty years, Peter Andrews created living soil that soaked up water and held it like a sponge. He found springs hidden under the dust and released the water to form streams and ponds where his horses drank their fill. He hauled in grasses, reeds and other plants to prevent the soil from washing away. With back-breaking work and lots of ingenuity, he transformed Tarwyn Park from a barren brown plot into an abundant patch of lush green, a haven for birds, butterflies and bees. His horses flourished, and he was a happy man.

Soon, he had visitors from around the country coming to him for advice. In 2006, one of those visitors was Tony Coote, a farmer whose land was all but lost to the drought. In one short year, in the middle of drought, Tony's farm was transformed. Tony saw the impact of Peter's wisdom and the potential for saving Australia's farms, so Tony and Andrew created a joint venture. Together, they helped farmers across their country to restore their fields.

Peter Andrews persevered in ways few people have the grit to do. As he neared retirement age, his End State seemed a sure thing, where he would spend his days enjoying his beloved horses as they thrived in the green paradise called Tarwyn Park.

Then, a coal mining company set their sights on Peter's sector of the country. One by one, they bought up the farms surrounding Tarwyn Park. The water became fouled, and the grass died. The

Andrews family ran out of options. They had to sell their beloved land. Within a few weeks, the mining company brought in heavy equipment, and thirty years of Peter Andrews's hard work disappeared off the face of the earth.

When I first heard this story, I thought, *What a tragedy.* Yes, the tragedy is real. The loss, the devastating grief is real. What happened wasn't fair or right. Most everyone would agree with that. But it happened. The only question left for Peter Andrews and his son was, "What's next?"

Before long, phone calls started coming in asking Peter to visit farms across Australia and around the world. People desperate to save their properties from drought called on Peter to bring his decades of experience to their areas, to help them restore their land. Tony Coote and Peter Andrews founded Muloon Institute to focus on research and gather data showing the best methods for restoring the soil and rebuilding the land. They needed data to convince lawmakers and skeptical landholders about the benefits of this new way of working with the land. Peter Andrews's focus expanded from Tarwyn Park to include the entire planet, and his influence continues to grow to this day.[49]

Behind every tragedy is a potential for bigger opportunities and greater influence. When the worst happened, Peter didn't close down and give up. He stayed open to expansion and opportunities. He took a Tactical Pause to ask, "What's next?" and he followed through.

After I came through my own Growth Opportunity in 2001, I thought my path to my own End State was settled. I regained my standing in the fire service and served for fifteen more years.

---

49   ABC News In-Depth, "Natural sequence farming: How Peter Andrews rejuvenates drought-struck land | Australian Story."

I immersed myself in studying leadership. I reached for my own potential, and I mentored others to find theirs. I worked hard to add value to others.

Over the years, I got complacent and was no longer mindful about my own wellbeing. I figured I was okay and didn't take the time for a personal Tactical Pause when I needed to.

"I got comfortable and didn't consistently check in on my own wellbeing."

The situation started out low key and comfortable when I reconnected with an old friend (I'll call her Charlene, not her real name), and we began dating. Because I had known her in the past, and we shared several close friends, I felt safe. Our relationship moved along much too quickly. She needed a place to live, so she and her young child moved in with me and my daughter.

I knew this was poor judgment on my part, but I ignored my misgivings. I should have stepped back and taken a breath to make sure my decisions were sound, but I didn't. I also didn't set my expectations with her as far as the bills and responsibilities were concerned. As a result, I began to feel a lot of financial stress that continued to grow worse as time went on until I ended up in debt.

During this same time, I was struggling with the symptoms of PTSD. To fill that bucket of stress a little more, I had three very traumatic calls on the job within the course of a few months—two gruesome murders and a young woman who burned up in a car accident. I knew they had affected me, but I didn't realize how bad my PTSD was. I wasn't sleeping. When I did sleep, I had nightmares. I wasn't thinking clearly at all. I felt broken inside, but my ego wouldn't allow me to admit I needed help.

My relationship with Charlene deteriorated to the point that I told her that I resented her and that we were finished. I plainly stated that she needed to move out. She said she didn't have a place to go and continued to live in my house. Resentment created a lot of pressure and stress inside of me. I kept shoving the discomfort down deeper and deeper to avoid confronting what I needed to do to resolve the situation. I knew what I needed to do, but I didn't want to face it.

One overarching theme throughout this period was that I stuffed down my painful emotions and feelings of self-reproach every time they tried to bubble up. I wasn't self-aware. I wasn't being honest with myself or others, and I surely wasn't defining my life.

At work, I was mentoring both men and women, some new to the fire service as well as officers. I was helping them establish both their professional and personal goals. I was also developing a mentoring program for women in the fire service. I saw the need to help women as I saw them struggle within the male-dominated system. I spoke to several female officers around the country asking for their support in a mentoring program specifically for women, and most agreed to participate.

At this time in my career, I was a Battalion Chief responsible for six fire stations. Every shift I would visit many, if not all of my stations. During one of my station visits I overheard a conversation that troubled me. It seemed as though a male firefighter had harassed a female firefighter. I joined the conversation, but it quickly went nowhere. I decided to ask several of the female firefighters I knew about inappropriate behavior toward them from their male counterparts.

Women began to confide in me about how a small percentage of male personnel habitually acted inappropriately toward female personnel with sexual statements, suggestive pantomimes and even groping them. I urged them to report this, but none of the women were willing to go on record and file a complaint. They felt that nothing would change. They would rather endure the sexual mistreatment than have the abuse escalate because they came forward.

I went to my shift commander and reported what I knew—I had a list of names and a list of actions. Unfortunately, I didn't know who did what. I had not witnessed anything, and the victims were unwilling to come forward. I felt that I had fulfilled my responsibility because I told my superior everything I could. I shared with him my belief that the policies in place did not protect females in the reporting process and created a culture where women felt it was better to endure than to come forward.

My shift commander went to his superior with the information. Over the course of several shifts, multiple meetings with leadership were scheduled, canceled and rescheduled. Those meetings never happened.

Leading up to this time, I developed a friendship with a young female fire fighter I was mentoring. She was also going through a breakup, and we started sharing personal stories. We played pool at a local bar, and I failed to maintain appropriate boundaries. Again, against my better judgment I crossed a line, tainting our professional relationship and elevating our platonic friendship to a romantic relationship.

I didn't notify my superior about the relationship because it was not clear how long it would last. I didn't want to complicate things in my life any more than they already were. She felt much the same way. Not reporting was against policy, but I figured it wouldn't be an issue and ignored it. If ever there was a time to take a Tactical Pause, that was it. But, again, I didn't want to feel uncomfortable, so I did what felt good and easy.

Charlene was still living in my house. When she discovered my new relationship, she confronted me, saying I was cheating on her. I again urged her to move out and an argument followed. She called 911 and accused me of domestic violence. Officers came to my house, arrested me, and I spent a night in jail. Ultimately, the charges were abandoned.

After my arrest, Charlene went to my employer and reported that I was in a relationship with another firefighter. What I thought would never come to light became part of a big investigation that cost me my job.

The charges of domestic violence had been abandoned. My relationship with a subordinate firefighter per policy would receive a written reprimand. The reason for my termination, from the paperwork I signed: I had not given my supervisor all the information I had relating to sexual misconduct toward women in the fire service.

Within days, my name was smeared throughout the media. The accounts seemed to insinuate that by reporting sexual harassment, I was trying to take the focus off my own misconduct and arrest.

After I had worked so hard to restore my good name, in a matter of days that was annihilated. My life's work was lost and worthless. At least it felt that way at the time.

Looking back, that year was a perfect storm. Events around me grew worse and worse because I didn't stop and get clear. I was in reactive mode and the worse things became, the more reactive I also became. Pride, ego, and desire were guiding my decisions. The further along things went, the more I stayed in a state of overwhelm.

When overwhelm sweeps in, all you can do is step back, take a breath and get clear. Course corrections are not always easy or pleasant, but the longer you wait, the more tangled situations become in your relationships, your finances and your career.

"Events around me grew worse and worse
because I didn't stop and get clear."

Once the termination papers arrived, I sank into a deep depression. I had disgraced my family name once again. I made matters worse by self-medicating with alcohol. I could not fathom a way out of the emotional pain and darkness that enveloped me. People I considered close friends levied contempt upon me, the whole spectrum from verbal criticism to complete abandonment.

After many of my friends cut ties with me, I drank to a new level of excess. I was past the point of caring about anything because I had ruined my life and damaged my most valued relationships. Talk about humble pie. I had to explain to my teenage daughter why I no longer held a respected place in my community. I had to explain why her friends might discuss the reasons her father was in the news.

I felt like I was broken, and I could not be fixed. On my way home from the bar one night after closing time, I decided to crash my truck. I unbuckled my seatbelt, rolled down my windows and accelerated to well over 90 m.p.h. I figured the wall I hit would most certainly kill me on impact. Rolling down the windows and unbuckling was to make sure it happened.

I looked up to the sky to ask for forgiveness for what I was about to do. Tucked into my visor is a picture of me holding my daughter on the day she was born. When I saw the picture, I slammed on the brakes, and everything went black.

The next morning, I woke up in my bed. My truck was in the driveway. Everything hurt because of my excessive self-medicating, but I wasn't dead. I sobbed, so ashamed of myself. I wanted to be better than I was, but I couldn't do it on my own. I had to be willing to get help and do the hard work in order to pull my life together. I had to take the Tactical Pause I should have taken months before.

Whether fair or not, regardless of who was right and who was wrong, the situation happened. I had to take an honest look at the conditions as they were in the aftermath of the crisis, take stock of what actions had been started and what actions I needed to take to restore order to my world.

Looking back over that year, I realized that as my challenges increased, I became more and more focused on the actions of other people and circumstances that were outside of my control. I focused on the second and third rings and didn't shore up the core, the things I could control. Instead, I looked for feel-good distractions that only made my problems multiply.

I did not have control of:

- What other people did or said
- Other people's emotions
- Decisions and actions taken by my superiors at work

I did have control of:

- My actions pertaining to my relationships, such as who was living in my house
- My finances, whether I allowed myself to go into debt
- My boundaries with my mentees
- Whether I followed my better judgment or not

When I sat down to write this book, I determined to be completely transparent about my own journey, because I know I'm not alone. Every great leader has experienced dark moments. Wise leaders stay humble because they know that their good reputation can disappear in the blink of an eye, whether they have been in their career for one year or for sixty years. They know that dark moments don't mean you are hopeless.

Even great people stumble. When you do, pick yourself up, learn where you went astray and get back in the game. Use your new wisdom to lift others up. Here are a few lessons that came from my most recent growth opportunity:

1. In the midst of making an important decision, if your pride, ego or desire to feel pleasure are driving the process, stop and ask yourself if feeling good for a brief time is worth losing everything you've worked so hard for. Ask

if your life's work is worth feeling uncomfortable a little while longer.

2. A mentor must set and maintain clear boundaries, regardless of the mentees gender.

3. Your reputation is fragile. Building and maintaining a reputation you can be proud of involves decisions you may have made many years ago. If you made some bad ones, they need to be addressed sooner rather than later when you can address them on your terms.

4. Feeling broken beyond repair is more common than most people think. Everyone goes through dark times. You are not alone. You can fix anything if you have the right tools and the willingness to use them. Your current pain could be the reason someone else finds help and hope.

As my life unraveled, I finally sought assistance for my mental health. I entered a program for PTSD and made some of the best friends of my life, people who truly understand and wholeheartedly support me.

During my healing process, I thought about what I loved most about my career and that was coaching and mentoring. So, I took more training, formed Hollenbach Consulting, LLC, and launched the "From Embers To Excellence" podcast. While I still coach firefighters, my focus has expanded to include clients in law enforcement and many other fields. I frequently receive invitations to speak about leadership. I get phone calls with new opportunities all the time.

When situations change, take time to consider ways around an obstacle or how you can take a completely new path. Situation changes could come in many forms:

- Burnout

- An accident
- A diagnosis
- Divorce
- Layoffs
- Lawsuits

Your purpose is bigger than your vocation. Your occupation is simply one avenue of expression for your life purpose in the midst of many possible avenues. Outside circumstances that move you from one job to another are redirections, not the end of the road.

When things fall apart, it's easy to get stuck thinking about what was instead of raising your eyes to the horizon and considering what could be next for you.

A Chinese parable dating back 2,000 years tells a story of a farmer and his son who make a living by growing produce to sell. The farmer has a horse that he and his son use to plow the fields and carry vegetables to market. One day, the horse finds a way out of the corral and runs away.

When the news gets out, many of their neighbors come to give their condolences on the loss of his horse. They know the horse is the farmer's prize possession, his only means of farming and taking goods to market. The farmer responds to their condolences by saying, "Who's to say if it is good or bad?" The villagers are impressed and somewhat confused at his indifference.

Several weeks go by. The horse returns, followed by several wild horses. The villagers hear of this windfall and return to celebrate the farmer's wisdom and good fortune. The farmer responds to their praise saying, "Who's to say if it is good or bad?"

A few days later, while breaking in one of the horses, the farmer's son is thrown and breaks his leg so severely that it appears he may lose the use of it, if not lose the leg altogether. The villagers know the farmer's son is his pride and joy, so they come to give their condolences and curse his bad luck. The farmer responds to their condolences saying, "Who's to say if it is good or bad?" The villagers are yet again impressed and somewhat confused at his indifference.

Weeks go by. The farmer's son is suffering a great deal. They hear news that war rages on the border of their country. The emperor's army comes to collect all of the able-bodied men to serve on the front lines. Because of his injury, the farmer's son is spared almost certain death. As you can imagine, the wise farmer approaches this with indifference, not knowing what the future holds. Who's to say if it is good or bad?

Your interpretation of a situation determines how you feel. How you feel determines how you respond. Whether an event is good or bad depends on your perspective, and your perspective is within your sphere of control. With a clear intention to remain humble, positive and grounded, you stay true to your values without going into reactive mode. You see the bigger picture.

You embarked on this journey because you are not average. You are anything but average, anything but ordinary. You endure things the average man or woman retreats from. You accept no excuse for mediocrity. When you stumble and fall on your face, you get up and keep marching because you know in your heart there is only one way to go and that's ahead.

The Man in the Arena

It is not the critic who counts; not the man who points out how the strong man stumbles, or where the doer of deeds could have done them better. The credit belongs to the man who is actually in the arena, whose face is marred by dust and sweat and blood; who strives valiantly; who errs, who comes short again and again, because there is no effort without error and short-coming; but who does actually strive to do the deeds; who knows great enthusiasms, the great devotions; who spends himself in a worthy cause; who at the best knows in the end the triumph of high achievement, and who at the worst, if he fails, at least fails while daring greatly, so that his place shall never be with those cold and timid souls who neither know victory nor defeat.

~**Theodore Roosevelt**, April 23, 1910 in Paris, France

AS A THANK YOU...

Download Your Free Grand Strategy Tools Today.

ABOUT THE AUTHOR

Retired Battalion Chief David Hollenbach is an experienced, decorated Chief Officer with a demonstrated history of working in the public safety industry in various capacities. He is skilled in Leadership Development, Emergency Management, and Disaster Response.

During his twenty-three-year career in the fire service, he served as a

- Firefighter
- Apparatus Driver/Pump-Operator/Engineer
- Company Officer/Lieutenant
- Battalion Chief in Operations
- Chief of Special Operations
- Critical Incident Stress Management (CISM) peer counselor
- Public Safety Rescue Diver
- Coordinator and developer of his department's first leadership development program

David Hollenbach is a veteran of the United States Navy with a Master's Degree in Public Administration from Barry University. A major focus of research for his capstone was how strong, positive leadership can influence the culture of a large organization.

While studying at Barry University he published "The Firefighter's Creed" and "Women in the Fire Service: A Diverse Culture Leads to a Successful Culture," an article highlighting the importance of gender diversity within the fire service in *Fire Engineering Magazine*.

He has spent years as an instructor, coach and mentor helping others define and realize success. He owns and operates David Hollenbach Consulting, LLC, and hosts the popular podcast "From Embers to Excellence." Although he no longer works as a servant to the community, his passion for service to others remains stronger than ever. For more information or to invite David to speak at your upcoming event visit www.HollenbachLeadership.com.

SOURCES

ABC News In-Depth, "Natural sequence farming: How Peter Andrews rejuvenates drought-struck land | Australian Story." Accessed August 31, 2021.

"About Daniel Goleman." DanielGoleman.info. Accessed August 31, 2021.

Ameli, M., & Dattilio, F. M. (2013). "Enhancing cognitive behavior therapy with logotherapy: Techniques for clinical practice." *Psychotherapy*. 50 (3): 387–391.

Aurelius, Marcus, *Meditations* 10:16.

Carman, John, and Anthony Harding, (ed.) *Ancient Warfare*, (Alan Sutton Publishing, 2002).

Chandler, D.L. "How Nelson Mandela refused freedom in 1985 before he walked out of jail in 1990." Face2FaceAfrica. com, Feb 11, 2019. Accessed August 31, 2021.

Dasgupta S (2004). *A History of Indian Philosophy*, Vol 1. New Delhi, India: Motilal Banarsidass.

Epictetus and James Harris. Epictetus. *The Enchiridion: Adapted for the Contemporary Reader,* Kindle Edition. (Independently Published, May 16, 2017).

"Five Communication Responsibilities." National Wildfire Coordinating Group. NWCG.gov. Accessed August 31, 2021

Fowler, Jeaneane (2002). *Perspectives of Reality: An Introduction to the Philosophy of Hinduism.* (Sussex Academic Press, Sept 1, 2002).

Frankl, Viktor. *The Doctor and the Soul. From Psychotherapy to Logotherapy.* (New York: Vintage Books, 2019).

Frankl, Viktor E. *Man's Search for Meaning,* Kindle Edition. (Boston: Beacon Press, 1997).

GoodReads.com. "Theodore Roosevelt > Quotes > Quotable Quote." Accessed August 31, 2021.

GoodReads.com. "Aristotle > Quotes > Quotable Quote." Accessed August 31, 2021.

Goodwin, Doris Kearns. *Leadership: In Turbulent Times*, Kindle Edition. (New York: Simon & Schuster, 2018).

Graver, Margaret, Edward N. Zalta (ed).»Epictetus.» *The Stanford Encyclopedia of Philosophy* (Summer 2021 Edition).

Hiriyanna, M. *Outlines of Indian Philosophy*, New Delhi, India: Motilal Banarsidass, 1993, reprint 2000.

Hollenbach, David R. III. "Women in the Fire Service: A Diverse Culture Leads to a Successful Culture." *Fire Engineering*, April 25, 2014.

"How to Be a Stoic: an evolving guide to practical Stoicism for the 21st century." howtobeastoic.wordpress.com. May 21, 2015, Accessed August 31, 2021.

Hulett, Denise & Bendick, Marc & Sheila, Y & Thomas, Francine & Moccio,. (2007). "Enhancing Women's Inclusion in Firefighting." *International Journal of Diversity in Organizations, Communities, and Nations.* 8. 10.18848/1447-9532/CGP/v08i02/39562.

Jones, Gabriel H. "Pythia." *World History Encyclopedia.* August 30, 2013. Accessed August 31, 2021.

Kulman, Linda & Henry Kissinger, *Teaching Common Sense: The Grand Strategy Program at Yale University*, Kindle Edition. (Easton Studio Press, LLC, June 7, 2016).

Plato. *Apology*.

Phillips, Stephen H. (2014). *Epistemology in Classical India: The Knowledge Sources of the Nyaya School*. Routledge Taylor and Francis Group, July 3, 2014.

Potter, Karl (2004). *The Encyclopedia of Indian Philosophies: Indian metaphysics and epistemology*, Vol 2. New Delhi, India: Motilal Banarsidass.

Ritter, Heinrich & Alexander James William Morrison, (1846). *The History of Ancient Philosophy*, Vol 4.

Seana. "Habit formation: Is 21 days all it takes?" Freeletics. com, 2016. Accessed Aug 31, 2021.

Walker, Ruby Jo. "Polyvagal Theory: informs all the work I do and teach." RubyJoWalker.com. Accessed August 31, 2021.

USNALeadConf. "USNA LC09 - Col. Arthur Athens, USMC (Ret.)" YouTube.com. Aug 26, 2013. Video Accessed Aug 29, 2021.

Van Natta, Matthew. *The Beginner's Guide to Stoicism: Tools for Emotional Resilience and Positivity*, Kindle Edition. (Althea Press, Oct 8, 2019).

Vidyabhushan, SC and NL Sinha (1990). *The Nyâya Sûtras of Gotama*. New Delhi, India: Motilal Banarsidass.

Vlastos, Gregory (1991). *Socrates, Ironist and Moral Philosopher*. (Cornell University Press, April 25, 1991).

"What Is Posttraumatic Stress Disorder?" American Psychiatric Association. Accessed August 31, 2021.

Wikipedia.com. "Sun Tzu." Accessed August 31, 2021.

A free ebook edition is available with the purchase of this book.

To claim your free ebook edition:

1. Visit MorganJamesBOGO.com
2. Sign your name CLEARLY in the space
3. Complete the form and submit a photo of the entire copyright page
4. You or your friend can download the ebook to your preferred device

A **FREE** ebook edition is available for you or a friend with the purchase of this print book.

CLEARLY SIGN YOUR NAME ABOVE

Instructions to claim your free ebook edition:
1. Visit MorganJamesBOGO.com
2. Sign your name CLEARLY in the space above
3. Complete the form and submit a photo of this entire page
4. You or your friend can download the ebook to your preferred device

Print & Digital Together Forever.

Snap a photo

Free ebook

Read anywhere

CPSIA information can be obtained
at www.ICGtesting.com
Printed in the USA
JSHW020427030922
30136JS00001B/9